CATFISH
The Three-Million-Dollar Pitcher

Also by the author

Parnelli
Mr. Clutch
Andretti
Great American Race Drivers
Life in the Pit
Clown
Confessions of a Basketball Gypsy
Vida
Stand up for Something
The Coaches
Emcee (Monty Hall)
Heroes of the Heisman Trophy
Champions of College Football
Classic Contests of Sports
Stars of the Olympics
The Walton Gang
Breaking the Game Wide Open
Foyt
Charlie O. and the Angry A's
Reggie

CATFISH
THE THREE MILLION DOLLAR PITCHER

BILL LIBBY

COWARD, McCANN & GEOGHEGAN, INC.
NEW YORK

For Matt Merola and Paul Goetz,
good businessmen, good men,
and good friends

Imperial Public Library
Imperial, Texas

SBN: 698-10736-5

**Library of Congress Cataloging in Publication
Data**

Libby, Bill.
    Catfish, the three-million-dollar pitcher.

    1. Hunter, Jim, 1946-   2. Baseball.   I. Title.
GV865.H85L52 1976   796.357′092′4   [B]   75-37643

Acknowledgments

The author wishes to thank Catfish Hunter and all the members of the Oakland A's and the New York Yankees for all past and recent interviews, as well as the publicity, public relations, and management individuals of both teams for all their help. He wishes also to thank Ron Bergman of the Oakland *Tribune,* Merv Harris and Glenn Schwarz of the San Francisco *Examiner,* Joe McGuff of the Kansas City *Star and Times,* Ben Olan of the Associated Press in New York, Chris Powell at the Ahoskie *Herald,* and other writers for their help, as well as Jim Roark of the Los Angeles *Herald-Examiner,* Russ Reed and Ron Riesterer of the Oakland *Tribune,* and other photographers for their contributions.

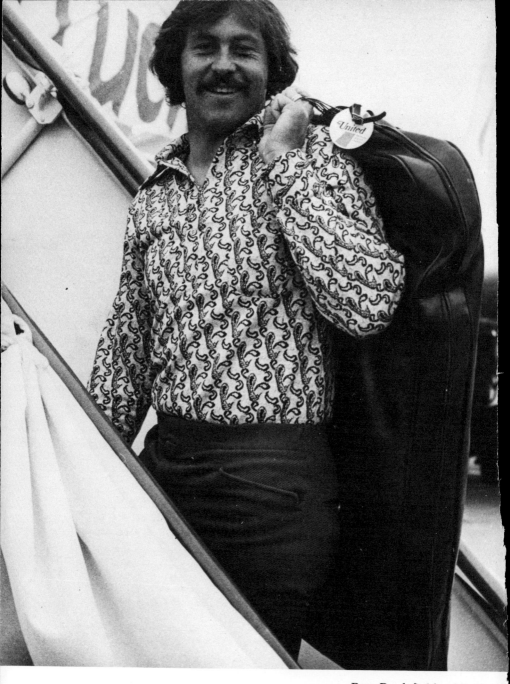

Russ Reed, Oakland *Tribune*

On his way, Catfish Hunter boards an airplane.

1

It was perhaps the most bizarre scene in baseball's 105-year history. They came from Los Angeles and Dallas and New York and points in between. A few flew in chartered and private planes and landed just outside of Ahoskie, North Carolina, at tiny Tri-County Airport, where the runways were barely long enough to accommodate their craft, but most made the trip in enormous jet airliners and landed at the larger airport in Norfolk. They drove in large rented cars across the Virginia-North Carolina line the 63 miles to this quiet town of 5,500 persons in the northeast portion of the state.

This is farmin' country. The visitors drove down U.S. Highway 13, "The Pleasure Route," past fields of tobacco, peanuts, corn, and cotton, through rows of towering pine trees, going for miles at a time without seeing a home or another person. They did pass the towns of Murfreesboro and Waylesville, and did see people working the fields. They passed farmhouses and barns. Inland there were streams being fished.

Not far from here are linen mills, located here because here they could be worked by cheap labor. Ahoskie has a textile mill, a tobacco warehouse, and ten churches. This is poor country. North Carolina recently was ranked forty-eighth among the 50 states in income. But it is beautiful country; it has its products and its pride. They like to call this "the Fertilizer and Herring Capital of the Country." They speak in soft, slurring, Southern accents of their love of the open life and how they would hate to be confined in the cramped cities of the North and East.

The natives regarded with wary amusement their visitors, the big-business men of baseball—the 50 to 60 team owners and chairmen of the board, the presidents and vice-presidents, the general managers and managers, the financial and legal advisers, dressed in expensive suits, wearing ties, carrying big briefcases, smoking costly cigars, and speaking hard and fast.

They came to town in waves for 15 days between the sixteenth and thirty-first of December, 1974, to bid from big bank balances for a precious piece of sporting property, James Augustus Hunter, known as "Catfish" in baseball, but simply as "Jimmy" in his home state of North Carolina, a nice-looking young man with a roundish, youthful face he has taken to concealing behind a flowing mustache and long hair in recent years.

Declared a free agent when an arbitration board ruled his Oakland A's contract invalid, Hunter had put his flesh on the block to go to the best bidder. The big-business men of baseball came from all across the country.

They gathered in their separate rooms at the Tomahawk Motel, figuring out the best bait to use to catch the Catfish, waiting their appointments with Hunter's representatives in the firm of Cherry, Cherry and Flythe, Attorneys, of Ahoskie, who handle his legal business.

"This helped our business quite a bit," admitted the owner of the 48-room motel, Mrs. Craig Vaughn.

The desk clerk, Clarence Godwin, commented, "They came down here, maybe two teams at a time, drivin' big ol' fancy cars, but they acted real nice. No wild parties, no broads. Didn't give us a lick of trouble."

They drove to the attorneys' offices in the Atlantic Farmers Bank Building at 119 Main Street, along an eight-block stretch containing three traffic signals, two restaurants, a bus station, and a few stores, along with railroad tracks, which intersect the center of town.

"Most of those baseball fellows, they all drove over there," noted Mrs. Vaughan. "It's only seven blocks away, but I didn't see any of them walk over there."

Every morning, Hunter himself would throw on his tan hunting jacket, stuff a handful of Red Man tobacco into his mouth, walk out of his unpretentious 10-room colonial house at his farm in Hertford, get into his muddy, gray pickup truck with a dogpen in the back and drive up the one-lane highway 45 miles to the meetings.

He'd find a place to park, pull a penny out of his pocket, and put it into a parking meter. This gave him an hour's parking without getting a ticket, but the meter would have to be fed hourly. Most of the meetings lasted one to two hours and there were two to four of them daily.

The backside of the building, along an alley, retained black stains on the faded red bricks from a fire which had forced remodeling inside.

Inside, the meetings took place in a plain room, 10 by 50 feet, with more than a thousand law books on four big shelves along the walls, and a greenish-gold rug on the floor. The groups sat along a plain, rectangular, brown table with ten plain green chairs, which were sufficient to seat Hunter, his four attorneys, the two to four representatives of each team, and a secretary, who took notes.

One of the attorneys, Earl Evans, described the setup as "conducive to eyeball-to-eyeball."

Hunter sat at a corner of the table, chaw in cheek, holding a Styrofoam cup into which he spat his tobacco juice neatly. J. Carlton Cherry, the senior attorney in the firm, took to keeping a chaw in his cheek, too, and holding a Styrofoam cup, into which he, too, could spit.

Said his secretary, Sharon Vick, "We hardly ever see Mr. Cherry with a chaw around the office, but he got swept up in the baseball fever and soon was chawin' like a madman, right along with the Catfish."

It was all low-key, but the amounts of money being discussed soon mounted into the millions, which was astonishing to the townspeople. Observed one of them, "Put all the working men in this town together and they don't make in a year a tenth the sort of money they are talking about at that table. Mebbe two years."

"It was unreal," admitted another awed resident. "Men who could buy and sell this entire town were walking our streets. It was like an invasion from Mars, sort of."

Waiting their turns, the baseball men wandered the main drag. Odom's Red and White was selling four cans of blackeye peas for a dollar, and hog jaws were on sale, but the visitors didn't buy a lot of these. They put coins in the soft drink machine at the gas station and sucked Cokes, and made small talk with the locals.

Gene Autry, the singing cowboy of old films and owner of the California Angels, stood on a street corner handing out free autographed record albums and shaking hands with old fans, who recognized his face, flusher and fatter than they remembered from movies.

Nearby, the town barber, Joe Andrusia, sat in his shop and grunted grumpily, "I wouldn't walk across the street to see Gene Autry." His chairs were empty, save for the one he was sitting in, as he listened to Elvis Presley and Johnny Cash records and gospel music on his radio and read a newspaper. "No one gets haircuts anymore," he complained. "They let their hair grow long like those baseball players do."

The news of the day was about the fire that destroyed Vann's Gin over in Murfreesboro, the robbery at John's Clothing Store, in which even the window mannequin was stripped of a suit, and, of course, the latest on the Catfish Hunter case.

Along with the baseball men, sportswriters and broadcasters came from the big cities to report the unprecedented proceedings here and they put up at the Tomahawk, too, but, unlike the baseball men, the media people griped about accommodations in the town.

"Where can you get a good meal in this burg?" they wondered.

Occasionally, they convened at the local newspaper, the Ahoskie *Herald,* which prints every Monday, Wednesday, and Friday, and has as its home a converted trailer with a makeshift sign nailed to the door, NEWS DEPARTMENT.

The Tomahawk Motel in Ahoskie, North Carolina, where visiting big leaguers berthed while bidding for Catfish Hunter during baseball's biggest-ever auction and most bizarre moment. Below: The main street, down which the men with the money went in pursuit of their prize.

Chris Powell, Ahoskie *Herald*

Chris Powell, Ahoskie *Herald*

Site of the pitches for the pitcher, the Farmers-Atlantic Bank Building, where Catfish Hunter's attorneys have their offices. Below: Three of his attorneys. Left to right: Ernie Evans, J. Carlton Cherry, and Thomas Cherry.

The receptionist, Jeanette Davis, is also the woman's editor, court reporter, and agriculture writer. The sports editor is a fifteen-year-old high school sophomore, Chris Powell. The local representative of the Associated Press, Ricky May, is, of course, older—sixteen.

"I guess," said Powell, "this has been the biggest thing here since that plane crash between here and Winton, which was before I was born."

"I'm the shortstop on the Ahoskie High School team," reported May. "Someday I'll get to play in the major leagues just like Jim Hunter.

"Only I reckon they won't pay me as much as they're gonna pay him," he added.

Patting their wallets and waving their checkbooks, the big-business men of baseball kept coming.

A woman at the Norfolk Airport car rental agency observed, "I had mo' folks, mostly middle-aged guys smoking cigars, asking for cars and directions to Ahoskie in one week than I've had in five years. What," she wondered, "was goin' on, anyway?"

This calls for some consideration.

Prior to the 1974 season, Catfish Hunter signed a two-year contract with the Oakland A's calling for a salary of $100,000 a year with half of each season's salary to be invested into a deferred payment plan.

According to Hunter, Finley agreed $50,000 annually was to be sent directly to an insurance company for investment. According to A's owner Finley this never was specified in the contract.

Reportedly, Finley balked when his advisers informed him such delayed payments could not be deducted from his income taxes as could the straight salaries paid most other players.

When Hunter was advised the payments were not arriving, he notified his attorney.

"At first, I thought all that was asked of me was an interpretation of a contract," comments J. Carlton Cherry, who had done other business for Hunter, but never had negotiated a baseball contract.

When Finley was advised he was considered to be defaulting on his contract, he was outraged. Charlie O contends he was perfectly prepared to pay his player. He offered it in cash to the Catfish, who turned it down.

Charlie O had opened a door through which Catfish was anxious to depart. The controversial owner of the A's was a domineering dandy who operated his empire with a heavy hand.

Although not one to hold grudges, Hunter held some against his boss. He felt he had been mistreated at times in the past, and he felt most of his teammates had been, too. And he felt he was underpaid, having signed his latest contract too quickly.

"I don't know what got into me," he said later. He did know that a lot of his teammates, none more valuable than he, were receiving much more, topped by Reggie Jackson's $135,000 contract. "Finley won't pay a player a penny more than he has to," observed Reggie.

Feeling Finley was defaulting on the contract, Cherry and Hunter first contacted Dick Moss of the Players' Association to inform him of the matter, which then was brought to the attention of baseball's brass. Finley may have felt he could break part of the contract without breaking the contract. He refused to pay as requested.

Bowie Kuhn, baseball's commissioner, but an old sparring partner of Finley's, could have ordered Charlie to pay, but did not. At this point, Cherry and Hunter determined to take the matter to court.

They announced the suit in Los Angeles just prior to the World Series. It might have been disrupting to team morale, but was not. The A's are used to disruptions. They went on and won.

"I'm not looking to stir up trouble. I just want what's comin' to me," Catfish commented.

Charlie shrugged it off, offering again to pay his pitcher in a pile of bills if necessary, and was rejected again. Base-

ball contracts were considered iron-clad. Charlie apparently figured he might have to pay the cash the way Hunter
wanted it, but he did not feel he would have to cough up the
contract.

The disputants agreed to settle the case in arbitration before a board baseball had been compelled to set up in recent
years to pass on player-management disputes. The board
consisted of three members—one representing the players,
one representing the owners, and a third who was agreed to
as a "neutral outsider." He was lawyer Peter Seitz, a professional arbitrator.

Jerry Kapstein, an attorney from Springfield, Virginia,
who had been handling contract negotiations for Rollie
Fingers, Ken Holtzman, Vida Blue, and other A's, was employed by Hunter and his hometown lawyer, J. Carlton
Cherry, to present Hunter's case. Neil Papiano, an attorney
from Los Angeles, represented Finley, although as usual
Charlie represented himself throughout the hearing.

Hunter raged later, "He didn't think I'd take the case to
arbitration. He wasn't gentleman enough to come up to me
and try to work things out. He was just trying to beat it
out of me. After the arbitration hearing, I knew I wouldn't
return to the A's because of everything he said there. He
just didn't show any appreciation for anything I'd done for
his team."

The case went to arbitration on the nineteenth of Novem-
ber in New York. The testimony was studied for nearly four
weeks before the vote was taken and the decision rendered.
As expected, the owners' representative voted on behalf of
Finley, the players' representative on behalf of Hunter.
The decisive vote then was cast by the neutral Seitz and it
went to Hunter.

He not only was declared a free agent, but Finley was ordered to pay the $50,000 as Hunter had wanted it, plus 6
percent interest.

When the panel ruled the contract to have been broken
and declared Catfish a free agent, the entire sports world
was surprised and Charlie was shocked, though not, never,

speechless. "The ruling is wrong," he raged, vowing to carry the case to higher courts although the arbitration by agreement was supposed to be binding.

Months later, even after Catfish had put on his new uniform and begun to perform for his new team, Finley insisted, "The courts will return my player to me and then there'll be hell to pay for all the games he couldn't play for us and all he played for the other team."

But, if he had paid the price for which Hunter had bargained in the beginning, even at the loss of a few thousand additional dollars in taxes, he would not have lost his star pitcher for even one season. And the cost in cash was not even remotely comparable to that offered the player by other teams.

When late in the 1974 season Catfish had confided to the A's player representative, Jackson, that he believed he could break his contract and become a free agent, Reggie wished him well and later wondered what the pitcher might be worth on the open market.

"A million dollars, maybe," he thought. At the time, others thought along the same lines, a million dollars being a nice round figure which remains impressive even in these days of inflated contracts. Catfish confesses he, himself, thought along these lines. "A million dollars is a mighty large amount of money," he admitted.

J. Carlton Cherry thought otherwise. The sixty-eight-year-old lawyer had never handled a million-dollar account, but long before the court case was settled he had begun to make discreet telephone inquiries across the country to determine the going rate for star athletes. He was surprised at the sums involved.

Because baseball had no rebel leagues to run up the bidding for talent, it had the lowest salary average in major league team sports.

The rise of the American Basketball Association had brought about a bidding war with the National Basketball Association which had driven the average annual award to players to a stunning $90,000.

The arrival of the World Hockey Association had brought about a bidding war with the National Hockey League which had shot average annual returns per player to $55,000.

The National Football League merged with the American Football League before salaries shot through the ceiling, but these nevertheless had risen to an average of $40,000.

Meanwhile, free from challenge, baseball's average annual payment per player stood at $35,000.

There were 50 pro basketball and 45 pro hockey players making $100,000 or more per season, compared to 30 in baseball.

Many athletes were making much more. Making moves or threatening moves to rival leagues rewarded hockey's Bobby Hull with $2,750,000 for 10 years and basketball's Kareem Abdul-Jabbar with $2,000,000 for five years.

Player agents pointed out they did not hold pistols at owners' heads, who would not pay these sums if they could not afford to pay. However, only those who could write it off against other profitable business ventures could afford it.

It was insanity, otherwise. Some owners have gone broke and some teams have gone bankrupt. Few operate profitably. Swept up in this insanity, men joined in the new World Football League and pledged payments they could not keep.

The most extreme madness came when unproven players were recruited at astronomical figures. On his potential, for example, Jim McDaniels was signed to an NBA pact for $2,100,000 for seven seasons strictly on potential and a season or so later he was playing in Italy and still being paid in the United States.

No unproven prospect, Hunter was the most consistent winner and the top pressure pitcher in his sport. Although a 10-year major league veteran, he was only twenty-eight. He had won 20 or more games for four straight seasons, including 25 the previous season. In this stretch he had won three play-off contests and four straight World Series decisions.

He was that rarest of baseball players—an experienced star at the peak of his skills who could be bought for cash. No top players had to be bartered in trade for him. No comparable players had to be awarded to his old team as compensation for another team securing his services.

This was by baseball standards a once-in-a-lifetime opportunity to pick up for money a player who had led teams to three straight titles. The one that did so would win favor with its fans by its willingness to purchase improvement. Ticket sales were sure to soar.

Were others of similar ability available often, the bidding would not have been anywhere as intense. They were not and at that time had not been.

So the big-business men of baseball left their concrete jungles and trekked to this wooden wilderness, invading this sleepy, small, Southern community to put in their pitches for this prized pitcher, and, as J. Carlton Cherry guessed, the least any of them was willing to offer was a mere million.

2

It was an auction of an athlete.

Jim Hunter was selling himself back into bondage. Regardless of fat financial rewards he may receive, the player really was forced to submit to a sort of slavery by the system of contracts Congress permitted major league baseball.

Through unusual circumstances, the Catfish had secured a release from his old contract. In the usual circumstances, he could not expect to again attain such a victory. The new club which held his contract would hold the rights to his pursuit of his profession.

He could farm for a living anywhere he wanted. Or raise hunting dogs. Or sell flea powder. But what he had that was worth the most, the ability to throw a baseball better than others, he would have to do for the team which gained his contract.

It could trade him to another team in another town at any time, and then he would belong to that team. It could bench him or demote him to the minors. So he would be a slave of sorts. And so he was not about to sell away his freedom cheaply.

So he made them sweat, the bosses of the teams that wanted him. And they all wanted him. He never before had made a big battle over a buck, but neither he nor any other baseball player now around had ever been in the position he was in—to demand top dollar.

Moreover, he wanted more than just money, though money could buy most of what he wanted. But he cared about other things such as preferable playing conditions, a strong supporting team, and long-term security for himself, his wife, and his two sons.

He sat down with his lawyers and they drew up a list of priorities. It was all very businesslike and so very unlike Catfish's conduct of his career in the past. His lawyers were J. Carlton Cherry, Cherry's son Thomas, their long-time partner, Joseph Flythe, and their new associate, Ernie Evans.

Although together they did not earn in an average year what their commission from this single situation would bring, these were no country bumpkins. They liked small-town life, made a comfortable living in their small town, and lived comfortably, but they impressed everyone with their shrewd, orderly approach.

The teen-age sports editor of the town newspaper observed that the outside media "made it look like Ahoskie is one of the all-time hick towns which happens to have a total of four smart guys—Hunter's attorneys." Observing them, no one doubted they were smart.

Ernie Evans laughed. "Well, we got a kick out of it. Ahoskie is a sort of a hick town. Being a hick isn't so bad. It's all in the connotation you put on the word. We're not big-city slickers. We weren't a bunch of sharpies out to outwit the other guys. We were doing a deal, driving a hard, but honest bargain."

At thirty, Evans was the youngest of the four attorneys who participated in the project. A newcomer from Wake Forest University, he also was the only mod member of the group, given to sort of fancy clothes, compared to the conservatism of the others. But he knew Hunter. He had batted against him in high school and caught him in American Legion ball.

"He was easier to catch than hit," Evans said with a grin.

J. Carlton Cherry at sixty-eight had practiced in Ahoskie for more than forty-five years and had done his first business with Hunter more than ten years earlier, though he had not been given a lot of business by the pitcher since. Carlton Cherry averages about $75,000 a year, so a lawyer can make money in Ahoskie, too.

His son, Thomas, forty-five, did about as well. So, too, did partner Flythe, forty-four.

They asked Catfish what he wanted from his contract, then told him what they thought he should have in it, and they discussed the types of teams he preferred. But, they agreed, whatever the team, its dollar-and-cents offer had to be at least one of the best bid, one which covered at least five playing years and could be spread out over many more years to provide protection for his family for the future.

Second, a club with a chance for the pennant was preferred so Catfish would not toil in vain. Third, an American League club was preferred because Catfish knew the hitters and knew he could handle them. Fourth, an Eastern Seaboard team was preferred so he could be fairly close to his home. Fifth, a club which played its home games on natural grass was preferred because it is kinder to pitchers than is artificial grass.

The lawyers lobbied on behalf of a New York or Los Angeles team because they believed he could benefit more from endorsements and other side monies here as he would not elsewhere. Ardently devoted to the hunting dogs he bred and trained, the Catfish confessed he'd always wanted to do a dog food commercial, so this thought turned him on a bit, but he had never wanted to live in a big city, so this turned him off a bit, too.

Los Angeles might not be so bad, he allowed, though it was a mighty far piece from home. He especially admired what he'd heard and observed of the Dodgers' organization, losers to the A's in the last World Series, but apparently a coming club. But he didn't like the thought of living in New York.

Well, he was advised, you can't have everything. He might have to pass up one or two of his preferences. It was the total package about which he had to be concerned most. And if it came from New York, he'd have to consider it seriously.

How much might that be in money? Catfish wondered. A

million? They smiled. More than that. Two? Closer to three, he was told. Maybe more than three. According to a friend the Catfish was stunned. It was simply so much it overwhelmed him.

A man who never wanted money to mean a lot to him, he started to think in terms of money being the most important part of the deal for the first time. "Someone in my family might finally be going to get wealthy," he observed wistfully. By today's standards, players are measured by the amount of money they make. Personal pride started to play a part in it.

Well, he'd always admired the Yankees, he admitted. He grew up while they were still the greatest team in the game, reading about all the great players they'd had when their team dominated the game even before he was born. Yankee Stadium always held a special attraction to him, he admitted.

But his attorneys did not want him to go into this thinking of one team over another. Let's see what they have to say, they suggested. And they contacted each of the 24 teams, inviting bids from each.

Commented J. Carlton Cherry, "We've told every club it has an equal opportunity, even Oakland, and that we'll do no horsetrading and make no special deals with any club. We are," he concluded, "interested not merely in money but the total package offered."

Added son Tom, "Whether it's for a few dollars or a few million, we always drive the best deal we can for our clients." Partner Flythe added, "It's not only salary and security Hunter has in mind, but living and playing conditions, too. Jim wants to go where he'll be happiest."

Unshaken by accusations that they were going to ask unreasonable amounts, associate Evans observed, "Our position is, if it was anyone else, they'd be trying to get as much as they could, too."

Like Robin Hood, they were ready to rob the rich to provide for the poor, though it certainly couldn't be called robbery, and the Catfish was far from poor.

Baseball, like other big-time sports, had become not only big business, but show business. However you set the stage, the one indispensable ingredient was the star performer. The promoter had to pay top dollar to get the top performer.

Perhaps at times they paid too much and failed to turn a profit. That was their problem. They had to draw the lines limiting their expenses to a figure with which they could live. The player had to live, too. The pie was there to be cut up. Each player wanted his proper piece.

Some teams drew lines. Some would not cross over these. Some would.

One baseball bigwig observed, "If there were a hundred Hunters, or even eight or ten available, none could command the sort of contract Catfish can. We in baseball would not want to bind ourselves financially or run the risk of going broke by bidding for stars the way the basketball and hockey owners have. We have been in a position to observe their idiocy from the sidelines and we're not going to act like idiots, too.

"The amount of money you're going to have to put up out front right off for him is minimal. Maybe you can write it off on taxes. Most of what you contract for can be spread over a period of years.

"And this situation has stirred up so much interest and he is so appealing a performer that you may come out ahead. Right off, he's going to increase season ticket sales. Then, for a while at least, he'll increase attendance on the days he pitches. This can mount up fast. And if he helps you win, he'll increase attendance that way too.

"No player brings with him the guarantee of your team's success. A player can get hurt or go bad overnight, anyway. But Hunter has been so consistent, he brings with him the probability of 20 victories a year, which might put you in the play-offs and World Series. And if he puts you there, his record shows he'll help you win there.

"If so, the value of your franchise would soar immediately.

"Some teams are in a competitive situation that he could

help. The Yankees and Mets in New York, the White Sox and Cubs in Chicago, the Angels and Dodgers in California, for example. If one gets him, the other team in the same town will be hurt more than anyone else.

"Finally, few teams can run the risk of not bidding for him because their fans expect them to go after the best. It is one thing to ask your fans to be patient because you have to build up a winner by developing stars and simply can't go out and buy top players, but it is another thing not to bid for the top player when one becomes available to be bought.

"Some owners are going to bow out of the bidding early because they can't or won't spend the sort of money needed to buy Hunter. They'll explain publicly that it is unreasonable to spend that kind of cash on one player who might get hurt or simply go bad, and it might cause unrest among their other players and be unfair to them.

"I don't think the fans will buy that excuse. Fans aren't reasonable. Fans are only interested in winning. They don't care how much money a player or a team makes as long as it wins. They don't care how interesting the games are, so long as their team wins. When you look like you're not doing all you can to win, you're losing your fans.

"They'll disguise the money paid Hunter in bonuses and side benefits and limit what they call his salary so as not to antagonize the other players, but the team that hooks the Catfish will have had to put a hell of a lot of bait on the line. But that team will win fans, even if they lose games. The least they will have done is show fans they were interested in winning at any cost, and the Catfish has become synonymous with winning.

"He won't win as much with others as he won with Oakland. Others aren't the Oakland team. He wasn't the only reason they won, you know. He carried them at times, but he was carried by them at other times. With him, they had the best team in baseball by far. Most teams he could make better, but not better than Oakland.

"Some of these other teams know this and they won't go to the limit to get him because of this. But they're sure as hell going to scream that they were screwed when they don't get him because they have to look like they gave it their best shot. There won't be many teams that won't at least pretend to try for him. And most really will try."

And who, he was asked, will get him?

"The Yankees, probably," he said. "They have the most going for them. The big city. The big rivalry with the Mets, bigger than ever now that they're temporarily sharing Shea Stadium. The big ballpark they'll have to fill when they move back into a rebuilt Yankee Stadium in a year or two. The big heat to be a winner again.

"But others will be in the running, too," he advised.

Originally, Hunter considered his old Oakland team a contender for his contract. "I would like to become a free agent and then come back with the A's. I'd like a long-term contract and a few other things, but I'd like to stay with them.

"It's like moving from one town to another where you don't know anybody. You'd rather stay in a town where you know everybody and where everything is. You know where to go to shop. You know where to go to eat. And everything," he said.

"That's the way it is with playing ball. You'd like to stay with the same team."

Despite his differences with his owner, he said, "I'll listen to Finley. The A's money is as good as any others."

Privately, he confided that he hated to look like he was deserting his teammates. He was told, "They understand. They'd do what they could for themselves if they were in your position."

He said they had won a lot together and he hated to leave a winner. He was told, "You can make another team a winner."

He pointed out they could make it four straight World Series victories. He was told, "Start a new string with a new team."

"It's not that easy," he said. And that 25-grand winner's share every year was nice. He was told, "You can't count on it with any team, not even the A's. And it's peanuts compared to the kind of cash you can pick up now."

Apparently the Catfish was convinced. Anyway, he got to feeling so good at being out from under Finley's heavy hand, he confessed, "I feel like I've been freed from jail." His former teammates sympathized with these sentiments.

The A's appeared to stay in the running to re-sign their ace for a long time, but they never really were in the running. Their only real hold on him was his loyalty to them, and once he lost his feeling for that, he lost interest in them.

A friend says, "Once the Cat decided he was not going to go back to Oakland, there was no way Finley was going to get him back. If they'd offered twice as much money as anyone else, he would not have gone back, and they didn't offer half as much.

"In the end, other clubs did offer more than he settled for, but other considerations swayed him."

With a winning team that wasn't making much money at the box office, always close with his cash, Finley was not about to match the multimillion-dollar offers of others for a pitcher he still believed should have belonged to him, anyway.

Besides, Charlie O believed he, more than anyone else, was responsible for his team's success. "We can win with Hunter or without him. No one man wins for us, unless I am that man," he said.

The A's, themselves, know how much Hunter mattered. Which was why Reggie Jackson put in a last-minute phone call to Hunter's home to try to sway the Catfish back to the A's. Jim was out, so Reggie spoke with Hunter's wife, Helen. She told him she was truly sorry, but Jim had made up his mind.

Reggie shrugged. He understood it. "The grass was greener elsewhere." He sighed. "Who wouldn't want him?"

Almost everyone did. The Giants, too, though they did not bid for him. A man trying to buy the Giants admits, "If we'd had the team, we'd have gone high to get him. It would have been beautiful. It would have burned the A's across the Bay. They would have been the team to have to leave town. Finley would have been ridden out on a rail. And we might have gotten him, because he was used to the Bay Area. But we hadn't gotten the team."

Horace Stoneham, who still held the Giants, but was trying to sell them, admitted, "We just can't afford to bid for Hunter." He already had unloaded most of his high-salaried stars from his financially troubled franchise and hardly could take on another one who would come higher than any of the others. So one team's best chance to win the Battle of the Bay went by the boards. The Giants were the only team not to enter a bid for Hunter. Some others now deny they did, but all did.

A few, such as Chicago's Cubs and White Sox and Minnesota's Twins, never were prepared to pay the price that the auction would produce. Minnesota owner Calvin Griffith, considered a close man with a dollar, anyway, and a man whose team was losing money in its town and might leave town, said, "It's a once-in-a-lifetime opportunity, but it could kill us. We'd like to buy Hunter, but we don't want to go broke." Before the bidding ended, however, he got sucked up into it.

Most spoke as if they would spend freely. Although Yankee owner George M. Steinbrenner had been suspended by Bowie Kuhn on admission of having made illegal political campaign contributions and was not supposed to participate in the operation of the team, general manager Gabe Paul later said: "When the Yankee partnership was created, George Steinbrenner publicly stated that everything possible would be done to provide a winner. He further told me we were not to back off in money deals.

"When his unfortunate suspension was invoked, he told me, 'Anytime you have the opportunity to buy the contract of a player for cash, I want you to go ahead whenever, in your judgment, it would be advantageous to the Yankees.'"

How provident this advice! So, the "silent owner" had been heard!

Others were heard, too.

"We want him. We'll try to get him," said M. Donald Grant, chairman of the Mets.

"We'll go as high as anyone," said Ray Kroc, the man behind McDonald's hamburger chain and the San Diego Padres.

"We'd certainly be willing to pay what he's worth," said Bob Carpenter, general manger of the Philadelphia Phils.

"We have no idea how much he's worth, but we are definitely interested in him. You have to be," said Boston Red Sox general manager Dick O'Connell.

"We're interested in all players with ability and he has ability," said general manager Joe L. Brown of the Pittsburgh Pirates.

"We would love to have him, and so would twenty-three other clubs," said Kansas City Royals' general manager Joe Burke.

Added Royals' owner Ewing Kauffman, "He could make the difference between winning and losing, and we want to win. We will pursue him vigorously, going as far and as fàst as we can."

Montreal president John McHale admitted, "We'll go high. I know that."

California Angels' general manager Harry Dalton said, "We'll be in there."

Added Los Angeles Dodgers' president Peter O'Malley, "We're certainly looking into it."

Texas Rangers' chairman Brad Corbett said, "We'll do what we can."

Phil Seghi, general manager of the Cleveland Indians, said, "We'll do everything we can do to get him. I think any team will. It will come down to which can do the most for him."

So the bidding began with baseball's wealthiest teams competing to see who could do the most for the Catfish.

3

The firm of Cherry, Cherry and Flythe, Attorneys, of Ahoskie, tried to conduct the negotiations for the services of Jim Hunter on a low key. Carlton Cherry, the senior attorney in the firm, says the visiting major league delegations did not seem distressed at the sort of terms that were suggested as appropriate for an ace pitcher's contract, but he admits he's not sure.

"Everyone was very pleasant," he says. "Of course what they said when they got back to their cars I don't know. They could have said, 'Wow, these hicks are really screwin' us good.'" He laughs.

As each of the teams gathered around the mahogany table in the Cherry offices, Hunter's lawyers laid out the sort of things in which their client was interested and then each team presented its proposals.

Each proposal was in a preliminary form. In high-dollar deals of this sort, you do not empty a bag of money on the table and say, "That's it!" Each side feels out the other to see how high the stakes will go. And no one was putting anything in writing.

All of the conditions in which the Catfish was interested had to be discussed in detail. Ways to work into the contract what could be worked in had to be worked out. Legal and financial experts had to be consulted. They speak in double-talk.

Daily for more than two weeks the stakes rose. As one team made a better offer, another topped it. Some teams decided they had gone as high as they could go, then decided to go higher. Some dropped out. Some dropped back in. They figured out new proposals.

It was the kind of negotiations which might have consumed many months, but Hunter made it clear he wanted the auction concluded as fast as possible. He was embarrassed by it, and he did not want it to drag far into the new year.

While the hunt was on for him, Hunter wanted to get back to hunting, back in the back country and out of the spotlight. "I really didn't enjoy it at all," he admits. "I had to do what was best for me. I had to do it. I didn't have to like it."

He was told not to talk too much to reporters, so he did not. He tried to keep a pleasant front for the townspeople. He did not want to make a big deal of the money with them. Most were old friends, for whom such money was beyond their wildest dreams.

The town's entire supply of 250 baseballs was bought up by the attorneys so the Catfish could autograph them and give them out whenever asked. But the invasion of one team after another kept him busy.

The Boston Red Sox delegation actually was the first to arrive at Ahoskie, on Dec. 18. Executive vice-president and general manager Dick O'Connell, vice-president Haywood Sullivan, and treasurer John Harrington represented Tom Yawkey's team.

Catfish recalled that in 1966 when he had to have an appendectomy in Boston, Yawkey had visited him in the hospital daily.

"He's a good 'man," observed Hunter, who after his experiences with Finley confessed concern about the type of people for whom he would now play.

Sullivan said of Hunter's crew later, "The fact that they are good honest people to deal with made it a good meeting. There's nothing really we can say until we hear from them again later, but they were forthright in letting us know in what financial areas they were looking to go, and I think we're prepared to go there."

The presence of the treasurer in their official party proved this.

Chris Powell, Ahoskie *Herald*

Manager John McNamara, left, and Bill Posedel, right, of the
San Diego Padres.

Chris Powell, Ahoskie *Herald*

Owner Gene Autry, left, and manager Dick Williams, right, of
the California Angels.

Manager Walter Alston, left, and president Peter O'Malley, right, of the Los Angeles Dodgers.

Fellow pitcher Gaylord Perry, left, pitching on behalf of the
Cleveland Indians.

Boston writer Peter Gammons observed that if the Red Sox line snared the pitcher, his nickname would be changed to "Codfish."

As had Cleveland and New York, Milwaukee also tried the personal touch by including player Mike Hegan, a former A's teammate of Hunter's, in the Brewers' official party, along with president Bud Selig, chairman Edmund Fitzgerald, and general manager Jim Baumer.

Hunter and Hegan got off in a corner and cut up old touches, old A's, and old man Finley.

The Dodgers not only were represented by president Peter O'Malley and vice-president Al Campanis, but flew manager Walter Alston down from his small hometown of Darrtown, Ohio, to chat with the Catfish.

"We talked mostly about hunting," Hunter said later of the visit.

Flythe smiled and said, "They talked about more than hunting."

The Dodgers later reported they never made an offer, but the Cherrys indicated that it was made clear to them that board chairman Walter O'Malley, still a power behind the throne, was willing to do business and wanted to be kept in the running until a final price was set.

Evans said son Peter O'Malley, the president of the team, "was on the phone with us on numerous occasions and told us how much he'd go up to." The Dodgers were prepared to break their long-standing commitment to one-year contracts to corral the Catfish.

Actually, the player-rich and fan-rich Dodgers, while needing another starting pitcher, were so confident they had constructed a club which could win several pennants in coming seasons and draw more than 2,000,000 fans each season that they did not seem to need Hunter as much as other teams might.

However, they wanted to remain in the running until they were sure their strongest rivals would not become stronger by acquiring him.

Cincinnati's Reds, the strongest rival to the Dodgers in

the National League's Western Division, dethroned by the Dodgers in 1974, were sure they could wrest divisional laurels back from L.A. in 1975, but dispatched a bid to Ahoskie.

They needed pitchers more than most teams, but had the power to overcome lack of pitching. A conservative club financially despite booming attendance, Reds' president Bob Howsam was not prepared to go as high as others for the pitcher. He never came close.

Another divisional rival, Atlanta's Braves, sent executive vice-president Eddie Robinson and manager Clyde King to make a pitch, but their low attendance and uncertain future did not permit the kind of presentation Hunter's advisers sought.

Still another, the Houston Astros, were in hot water financially. Their owner, Roy Hofheinz, had a shaky hold on his team, and the job of his general manager, Spec Richardson, was in jeopardy. They asked what Hunter wanted, then decided they would not stay in the bidding.

The Baltimore Orioles were on the block. Owner Jerold Hoffberger and executive vice-president and general manager Frank Cashen conferred with Catfish's forces, then looked for the door.

Swiftly the Orioles, Astros, Braves, and Reds had joined the Giants on the sidelines.

Another financially troubled team, Chicago's White Sox, who had a small park and weren't filling it, had just disposed of high-salaried Dick Allen and were interested in disposing of their entire franchise. They displayed a curiously reserved interest.

"We're not going to enter into a bidding war for Catfish Hunter," declared owner John Allyn. "If Mr. Hunter has any interest in pitching for the White Sox, we surely will be happy to listen to what it will take, but I don't want any part of playing one offer against another."

Added general manager Roland Hemond, "We feel sincerely sorry for Mr. Charles Finley's position in the situation."

At the time Mr. Finley was involved in a three-way deal to place his A's in Chicago and transfer the White Sox to Seattle. It would not materialize.

Hunter had less interest in pitching for the White Sox than the White Sox did in paying him what it would take to get him to pitch for them. After the White Sox discovered in a telephone conversation what it would take, they joined the A's on the sidelines.

Finley had phoned in a bid, but it didn't come close to what the Hunter forces sought, who were not feeling sorry for Charlie.

Chicago Cubs' owner Phil Wrigley asked his general manager, John Holland, to contact Catfish's attorneys at once, but never dispatched a delegation, was not agreeable to the sort of terms mentioned, and swiftly joined those out of the running.

The Detroit Tigers tendered a bid, but were told it fell far short of others, so they tucked their checkbook away. A representative of the team said, "The kind of contract they want is way out of line. If he hurt his arm tomorrow we'd look like the village idiot."

As the bidding boomed past the one-million-dollar level, a number of teams clearly were willing to take that chance. New York's Yankees and Mets, California's Angels and Dodgers, the Minnesota Twins, Texas Rangers, Boston Red Sox, Cleveland Indians, Montreal Expos, Kansas City Royals, Pittsburgh Pirates, and Philadelphia Phillies all remained in the running.

Gussie Busch's St. Louis Cardinal delegation, headed by executive vice-president and general manager Bing Devine, pitched a $1,000,000 bonus and $175,000 yearly salary for five years—a $1,875,000 package. When they were advised that was not enough, they decided they'd gone far enough, and retired.

Nor were the Mets willing to go past $2,000,000, despite annual attendances topping 2,000,000 fans. Perhaps they considered their support stable and did not see how Hunter could add to their income. They tried to reason with the

Catfish's crew, stressing side monies to be made in New York.

M. Donald Grant, chairman of the Mets, offered a $1,000,000 bonus and $150,000 yearly starting salary on a contract to be renewed a year at a time. He pointed out that if Hunter took his million in cash, used half of it to pay taxes, and invested the other half in tax-free bonds at 7 percent interest, it would have been built back to the original million within 10 years. And it would be worth 1½ million within 15 years, before Hunter was forty-five. And all his taxes on the money would have been paid.

Hunter's forces were willing to acknowledge such a program might work, but they wanted more. Because the offer came from New York, they were willing to negotiate further. One of the suggestions Hunter's attorneys had made to him was that rather than subtract all of their fees from his share, they should simply ask a substantial sum to be used toward this as part of the total package, and that it would not be so substantial anyone would risk blowing the deal because of it.

The Mets were willing to go for $200,000 extra in attorneys' fees. Rather than add more to their package, they offered to loan Hunter another $250,000 to purchase land he wanted to buy adjoining his farm, the money to be repaid without interest from earnings from his farm.

They would not guarantee Hunter a long-term contract at $150,000 a year, but had worked out an elaborate table by which if Hunter won 25 or more games his salary would increase by 10 percent to $165,000 for the following year, or if he won 30 or more by another 10 percent to $180,000, but if he won less than 20 it would decrease by 10 percent to $135,000, and if less than 15 by another 10 percent to $120,000.

A Met spokesman said, "We've about had it with long-term contracts at guaranteed prices. Our experience with Rusty Staub and others leads us to feel these destroy incentive on the part of the player. You can't commit yourself beyond performance. On the other hand, we feel contracts calling for automatic increases or decreases pegged on performances are reasonable.

"We're happy to pay one hundred and eighty-five thousand dollars for a thirty-game winner, but why should we pay one hundred and fifty thousand for a ten-game winner? If he continues to produce his value to us, his contract will continue to increase. If he doesn't produce, his cost to us is decreased in proportion to his value to us. It seems reasonable to us."

The Hunter forces found this not only unreasonable, but insulting. They felt Hunter's consistent record of success supported his desire for a guaranteed income over a prolonged period. His history indicated he never had tried to renegotiate an unexpired contract on the basis of his success. They felt he had earned protection.

Negotiations with the Mets were broken off.

The Montreal Expos' expeditionary forces, headed by vice-president Jim Fanning, pitched a package worth $1,500,000, plus an insurance program with the payments to be spread out over a prolonged period. It amounted to about $2,000,000, but when that turned out not to be enough, they withdrew from contention.

Fanning said, "We're starting to lose our heads."

Minnesota also dropped out at about the $2,000,000 level, too. Owner Cal Griffith said, "Even though we were prepared to go as high as two million, we found after discussions with Hunter and his attorneys that we weren't even in the ball park." He heaved a sigh of relief. His economic condition did not allow for this sort of expenditure.

The California Angels dropped out at the $2,000,000 level. General manager Harry Dalton said, "I made what I felt was a sensible offer. We didn't think going to three million was sensible."

Owner Autry packed up his remaining record albums and they headed home. "I don't want to look like a fool in front of the other owners," he said. "The figures are getting out of hand and could ruin baseball. If we pay him this, what are we going to pay others of equal value?"

The Angels had one—Nolan Ryan. Dalton noted, "If Hunter is worth three million, Ryan is worth four million."

Autry had paid only $2,100,000 for the entire California franchise less than 15 years earlier.

The Texas Rangers dropped out at the $2,500,000 level. Owner Brad Corbett commented, "We made them what we thought was a very substantial offer. But they told us it wasn't substantial enough. We told them we just couldn't do any more. There comes a time when you have to think about what's best for your ball club as a whole. There are twenty-five other guys to worry about, too.

"Boston has the best chance," he concluded.

Texas Ranger general manager Danny O'Brien added, "Maybe we still have a chance. We left the offer lying there on the desk. Maybe we'll hear from them yet." They did not. They had no chance. They were out of it.

Montreal, which had dropped out, had worked out a new package based more on deferred future income than present payments. It also amounted to about $2,500,000. Through general manager Fanning they also had left it lying there. "As far as we know it's still on the table," he said. But it had been brushed off.

Atlanta also reentered with a revised set of terms that amounted to about $2,500,000. This apparently was the line many serious bidders had drawn as their limit. Executive vice-president Eddie Robinson sighed and said, "We've gone as far as we can go." It was not far enough. They, too, were removed from the running.

The Phils dropped out at around $2,600,000. They stretched their limit a little. When it wasn't enough, they went on their way. "I'm shaken," said president Ruly Carpenter. "I could not go any farther.

"We have been taking a long, hard look at the situation, but have decided not to make another offer. There comes a point at which reason has to prevail."

Passing this point, the remaining contenders—the Pittsburgh Pirates, Cincinnati Reds, Los Angeles Dodgers, San Diego Padres, Boston Red Sox, Kansas City Royals, and

New York Yankees—were wary and restless, worried if they were not, indeed, going too far.

Observed one of the contending executives, "I think at this point some of us are scared we will win. We're getting carried away, inching our offers up past reasonable points. Maybe we're looking good to our fans and maybe by now that's really all we want. It's one thing to bid this kind of cash, but it would be something else to have to pay it."

Concluded another, "The inmates have taken over the asylum. This is madness. No player is worth this. He's not Cy Young. He's not Walter Johnson. And they wouldn't be worth it. Babe Ruth wouldn't be worth it. We're so busy trying to outbid one another we've forgotten what we're bidding for. We've forgotten who Catfish Hunter is. He's a good pitcher. Maybe the best. But he's not that good. No one is."

Who was he, then? How good was he? As the bidding in this bizarre auction approached $3,000,000 one had to wonder what had brought baseball and this pitcher to this most curious of crossroads in the sport's history.

4

When Jim Hunter returns home to Hertford each winter, he always looks up his grade school teacher, Mrs. Jay Dillem. She always used to tell him, "You're going to have to study, James Augustus. There's not any money in baseball."

She doesn't know what to say now. But, back when Jim was beginning, few people believed baseball would be his way to a fortune, few in that small farming community thought of fortunes, most felt you had to work hard for any money you made in life.

He was born in Hertford on April 8, 1946, less than a year after World War II ended, the youngest of nine children—five sons and three daughters—born to Mr. and Mrs. Abbot Hunter, straight, simple people who believed in hard work and a good, decent family life.

Now retired, Abbot Hunter was a tenant farmer who scratched a living out of the earth and used to hustle logs on the side for extra money at $2 an hour. He worked hard, dawn to dusk, and never came close to earning $10,000 a year in his life. But he made enough to raise his family properly.

Marvin, the oldest son at forty, now is the Hertford town clerk. Pete, thirty-two, is a driving instructor and baseball and basketball coach at Perquimans High School. Edward works for the state highway department. Ray works Jim's farm. All the Hunter children, married and with children of their own, still live in the Hertford area. They have ties there they find they do not want to cut.

They all had chores to do on the farm and in the house

Russ Reed, Oakland *Tribune*

The young A's pitcher keeping track of pitches and balls in the
dugout during a game.

while they were growing up. Before he went to school in the morning, for example, Jim had to get up at 4 A.M. to feed hogs and milk cows. After school he sprayed peanut crops, harvested corn, and loaded melons on trucks.

But his father, a former catcher in sandlot games, always let his sons off to play their games, and they played football, baseball, and basketball on almost all levels as they grew up.

Jim recalls one day when there was no school he loaded watermelons from sunrise to midnight, then pitched the following day. He says he was stronger at the age of eighteen then he is today. He also says he hates watermelon to this day.

In their spare time they did a lot of hunting and fishing, but played a lot more ball. "We played, rain or shine," Pete Hunter recalls. "When it rained we went to the barn and broke up corncops and tried to hit them with sticks. We just pitched and hit and raised the devil. One of us would try to throw those cobs by the others. One of us would have to strike out the other three times. Jim could do it a lot, but so could I." Jim used to practice by throwing the cobs through a hole in the barn wall.

Francis Combs, his high school catcher, says Jim always was practicing. "I lived in town, but sometimes I'd go over and spend the weekend with Jim on the farm. He'd pitch to me for the weekend. He was big and strong from doing the farm work and he was always working and getting better."

Jim's brother Pete preceded him as the hurling hero of Perquimans High. "As a junior, I pitched my first perfect game, against Camden. Later, Jim pitched one, against Elizabeth City. When Jim came home the afternoon he pitched his, he said, 'You don't have anything above me now,' and I knew just what he was talking about.

"Then he said, 'But I didn't strike out fifteen, like you.' He struck out ten. That's the only thing we compared. I had him there.

"I was good. My senior year I was eighteen and three and I finished every game I pitched," Pete proudly recalls. "But

Jim was bigger and better than I was. I'm only five eight today, and he's six foot. Maybe I envy him some, but I'm happy for him," says Pete, who earns $13,000 a year coaching other kids in the same school he and brother Jim attended.

Jim was 26–2 his last two years in high school, he pitched that perfect game the day following Easter Sunday, 1963, and five no-hitters in all, and he struck out twenty-nine batters in a 12-inning game.

Floyd "Dutch" Olafson, a former ballplayer who served as one of the "bird-dog" scouts who covered an area of small towns, spotting talent the big league scouts might want to see, says, "The first time I saw Jim pitch, I knew he'd make the major leagues. He throwed smoke then. I was the first scout to see him, when he was a sophomore, and I told the big scouts about him, and after that everyone was interested in him."

Jim's catcher, Combs, recalls, "In high school, Jim just overpowered everybody. He had a good curve, but he didn't have to throw it. I'd give him one signal for a rising fastball and one for a sinking fastball. Tommy Byrne—I think he was scouting for the Yankees—came through and worked with Jim during his junior year. Taught him the rising fastball and the sinking fastball. I think he can still throw both, depending on how he holds his fastball now. Maybe it just seemed so to us then, but he was faster then than he is now, or maybe was after his accident."

In Hertford, the Combs family is almost as well known as the Hunter family. Fred Combs became an All-American defensive back in football at North Carolina State, and Francis Combs was considered a pro baseball prospect as a catcher at the same time Jim Hunter was being scouted as a pitcher. Francis signed with the New York Yankees and played in the minors at Johnson City, Kinston, and Fort Lauderdale before he gave up baseball.

"I realized best I'd ever make would be maybe Triple-A, so I quit," he says. "Now I'm an industrial supply salesman in Raleigh and my major league baseball is following Jim Hunter. My wife and I went out to visit him in California.

Still the same good guy, still the guy who lets me come to Baltimore when his team is there so I can pitch batting practice and be with the big leaguers.

"He's a great guy, not like a lot of people who get big-headed. Same old Jim Hunter. I'm sure he signed with the Yankees because he wanted to be closer to home. Whenever the A's came to Baltimore, he'd pitch, then come home a couple of days, and then join the team in Cleveland or New York or Boston. Any chance to come home, he'd come home. Same guy he was in high school."

"I don't know if Jim did it for that, but it's great that Jim signed with an East Coast team," brother Pete enthuses. "Now we've got half the season to go up and see him pitch some games and we don't have to go far. Going to California—well, that was a special trip. And we couldn't always make it when he'd come East for a few days at a time."

"Knowin' Jim, maybe he did have that in mind."

Bobby Carter coached Jim in baseball and football at Perquimans High, though he now coaches at Roanoke Rapids High, 38 miles away. "More opportunity here, but no Jim Hunters," he says with a sigh.

"Jim was an outstanding all-around athlete. He was just a big old country kid who loved it rough, so he made a fine football player. He played defensive linebacker and offensive end as a starter for three years. Jim loved to hit, loved to mix it up. He'd have been a good college football player.

"But baseball was his real love. Course, he started for me for four years in baseball. As a freshman he played the outfield and infield. Played some first base. We needed his bat so we had to have him in there somewhere. As a sophomore, he alternated between shortstop and pitching. He'd pitch or Fred Combs would pitch. As a junior and senior Jim was our top pitcher, of course."

Originally a sidearmer, Jim started to throw overhand his last two years in high school at the suggestion of scouts and his coaches.

During his junior year big league scouts filled the stands wherever Jim pitched and there was a lot of talk that after his senior season he could command a bonus of $100,000 to $200,000.

That was the last year before the drafting of amateurs by big league ballclubs and any team still could sign any player, and teams went high to sign the top prospects. That's when Charlie Finley built the base of his championship clubs, outbidding others for kids of potential, and not having to wait his turn to take what was left as the draft rotation proceeded.

But Jim Hunter's dreams of a professional baseball career almost came to an end in the fall of 1963. It was Thanksgiving Day and he had helped his high school team to a football championship that day. The brothers Jim, Pete, Ray, and cousin Alton Stallings went hunting happily later that day.

As Pete recalls it, "We went to the canal at Bear Point, which is right where Jim's home is now, about six miles outside Hertford. Ray and Alton went on up ahead. When Jim and I saw some ducks flying, Jim went ahead to shoot, but when I went to shoot my gun, a twelve-gauge shotgun, misfired.

"I loaded up again with buckshot. As we were walking along I had my gun pointing at the ground, but it went off. When it did, it got Jim right in the right foot. He fell right into a ditch.

"I asked him what had happened.

"'You shot my damned foot off,' he said."

As Jim recalls it, "I saw holes in my boot. Then blood started coming out. 'Damn!' I said."

"We were a mile from anybody's house," Pete remembers. "Alton went up to my brother-in-law's house to get a truck. But it was too wet, the area had just been plowed, and we couldn't use it. We had to carry Jim by hand across some real wet farmland.

"We drove him to a hospital in Chowan, fifteen miles away. He was in pain, crying. We got him to the emergency room, where they took care of him."

Jim lost the little toe on his right foot, the use of the toe next to it, and partial use of the next two. Doctors sewed up the stump and extracted about 15 pellets from the foot. They bandaged him up and sent him home, hobbling on crutches.

Jim thought his baseball was behind him. He started to think of going to East Carolina College instead. His family, especially Pete, of course, was deeply disappointed and felt sorry for him. Jim felt sorry for himself. Pete felt guilty. "Jim insisted it was just an accident, but I don't know if I'd ever have forgiven myself if he hadn't overcome it," Pete says.

Jim did overcome it. He was on crutches most of the winter, but he was off of them in time to come back the following spring for his high school senior season of baseball. His foot hurt a lot and he was to pitch the first few games before he was able to get his form right, but once he started to pitch again, he pitched well. He compiled a 14–1 record and hurled his school to the state championship.

"I told my daddy that if I could walk again, I'd pitch again. I was very determined," Jim recalls.

Charlie Finley flew in to see that game. He liked what he saw. Afterward, accompanied by a police escort, he drove to the Hunter farm in a long, black limousine, followed by a smaller car full of aides. They disembarked and descended on Hunter and others there the way small children fall on their presents around the tree at Christmas.

"Nothing like that had ever happened in Hertford before," Hunter recalls. "Mr. Finley started passing out green warm-up jackets and green bats and orange baseballs."

He suspects it scared off some scouts, who thought Finley had him wrapped up for delivery to Kansas City, where the A's were playing at the time. "A Detroit scout told me they would never have let me go, but for my foot," he says. However, he admits they also were scared off by his loss of speed.

"My senior year record was fine, but I wasn't able to throw the ball as fast as before the accident. In fact, I never have been able to. They saw that. I think they also were worried I'd develop an unnatural motion to favor my foot and I'd hurt my arm. Some of them warned me about that.

"Most of them seemed to lose interest in me. Most of them stopped coming around to see me. Finley left and didn't come back. I started to lose hope."

But Clyde Kluttz, scout for the A's, and a couple of other scouts still saw hope for his future. Clyde recalls, "A lot of people were worried that his career was over before it started, but I wasn't. I knew Jim. I knew what he could do. I knew what a competitor he was. I told Mr. Finley I still wanted to sign him. He said to have Hunter call him and he'd talk terms with him."

Based on a tentative offer from a New York Mets' scout, Hunter asked Finley for a $50,000 bonus and the promise of an additional $25,000 to cover a college ecucation if he didn't make it and decided to go to college later. Finley agreed on condition Jim would be examined by a doctor and declared fit to play. Hunter agreed on condition Finley threw in a new car.

"I wanted a new car real bad," he recalls.

Finley did not agree to this. It meant only a small addition to the amount he was willing to spend, but when Finley figures he has gone as far as he wants to go, he can be stubborn. He held Hunter on the telephone line for four long hours arguing the point with the youngster.

As Hunter remembers it, "Finally I told him to give me two hours to call up the other scouts to see if they'd top his offer. But that kinda angered him and he said if I didn't agree now, he'd cancel the offer.

"I knew the Mets' scout had been unable to reach his boss to approve their offer. I didn't know if they'd go for the car, either. I told my father, whispering, what Finley had said. He shrugged and said, 'It's your decision.' I was scared.

"Well, seventy-five thousand dollars was more money than I'd ever thought existed before, so I said I'd take it."

He still refers to the bonus sum as $75,000, although as

Clyde Kluttz points out, since Hunter never took advantage of the college provision in his contract, Finley actually only spent $50,000 on the bonus.

Hunter recalls, "Clyde Kluttz came by with the papers and I signed in front of my mother and father. No writers. No cameras."

But before Finley would pay anything, Hunter had to go to the Mayo Clinic in Rochester, Minnesota, to have his foot examined. Here they discovered many remaining pellets and decided to remove most of these, surgically. The few they could not reach without risk to his use of the foot they decided to leave in.

These remain in the foot and Hunter says they sometimes still bother him. However, he recalls, "The doctors told me the best thing to lose on your body if you have to lose something is your little toe. You don't need it. Being in my right foot was a break. That's the foot I push off. It would be worse if the problem was in the foot I land on. They said I probably could pitch as well as ever."

Finley later contended he had taken a chance in giving Hunter his chance, pleading that this reinforced his right to the pitcher.

Hunter, however, disputes this: "If the doctor had said I wasn't all right to pitch, then Finley didn't have to pay the bonus."

Reportedly, when Finley found out doctors had to take more pellets out of Hunter's foot and leave still more in during the examination, he tried to cancel the deal. He sent to baseball's minor league office to have the contract returned to him before it was approved, but it had been sent to the major league office and was approved before he could get it back. Thus he was stuck with it.

Finley invited Hunter to the owner's farm in La Porte, Indiana, to collect. Driving there, the first thing he saw was a huge white barn with a green *A* set against a baseball painted on the side. At night, lights illuminated the *A* so it could be seen for miles.

Hunter remembers, "When I went through the gates, I

thought the tenants' quarters were Mr. Finley's house, and that his house was some kinda motel. I never saw a house so big before. I got lost in it right off.

"I was back on crutches and I spent a good hour hobbling from room to room trying to find my room.

"Eventually I went out to the barn where Mr. Finley had installed a basketball court on the second floor. A bunch of Kansas City players were playing basketball there.

"Ken Harrelson was running around in his underwear in front of some of the other players' wives. I was shocked. It was something I would never have seen in Hertford. It was the beginning of a whole new life for me.

"Harrelson almost ran over me on a fast break and growled, 'Get outta the way, boy, you might get hurt.'

"I said, 'Yes, sir,' and hobbled out of the barn. The whole scene there was something I never forgot.

"I finally found Finley and, of course, once you meet him, he's someone you'll never forget.

"It was all quite an experience for an eighteen-year-old farm boy," Hunter says with a smile.

Harrelson, of course, preceded Hunter as a free-agent escapee from Finley, who signed with another team for a lot of money, though nowhere near what Hunter received when his auction was held.

Ten years later, following the New Year's Eve signing ceremonies with the Yankees in New York, Hunter said he had to hurry off to catch a plane for home and nothing could stop him from keeping his dawn date with his father.

"What if one of your toes is shot off?" a wise guy asked.

"I'd make it on eight, then." Hunter laughed. "After all, I've been doing just fine on nine."

5

James Augustus Hunter had no nickname when he signed with the A's. His new owner is a man who considers nicknames a colorful part of the players he is trying to sell to the public. According to Jim, Finley asked him if he had a nickname, and when he told the owner he did not, Charlie was disappointed.

"You're sure?" Charlie asked again.

Jim Hunter said he was.

"Well, then I'll think up one for you," Charlie said.

He asked Jim if there wasn't anything unusual he liked to do or anything like that.

Brother Pete piped in, "He likes to fish. He catches a lot of catfish. When Jim was a boy he wouldn't eat any fish except catfish."

"That's it," Charlie said. "We'll call you Catfish. Catfish Hunter."

And with that, he announced the signing of a prized schoolboy, "Catfish" Hunter, to the press and public.

Finley figured out a story for Jim to tell whenever asked about his nickname and for many years Jim dutifully did as he had been asked to do. When asked, he would say it stemmed from a time he had run away from home as a boy, gone fishing, returned with a catch of catfish slung over his shoulder, and had the nickname ever since.

Now, he says, "I did fish a lot as a boy, but I didn't think much of my new name. But I also didn't want to cross this man who was spending so much money on me, so I said all right. I didn't think anything would ever come of it. I didn't think the name would stick. I just didn't think. The name stuck.

"No one knows my real name anymore. But that's OK because no one would know me as well as they do if it wasn't for my nickname now. 'Catfish' is colorful and because of it I became famous fast.

"Ask someone sometime who Jim Hunter is. Still, I'd sort of like to hear it sometimes. The only place I hear 'Jim' is at home. That man sure can change a man's life around."

Charlie O couldn't talk all his players into using nicknames, but Johnny Odom became "Blue Moon" Odom, for example. And when Vida Blue burst on the scene, Finley made him an offer. As Vida recalls it, Finley said, "Baseball is a business and we have to sell. People buy colorful personalities. A colorful nickame will help you. An unusual name will help you even more. Why don't you change your middle name to True? We'll call you True Blue. It's a natural. We'll tell our broadcasters to call you True Blue. We'll even put TRUE on the back of your uniform. How's that?"

Vida said he was startled, taken aback. He said later it reminded him of plantation owners who gave their slaves any names the owner fancied. But he was not rude. He simply said, "No, sir, I don't think I'd want to change my name." Finley persisted: I'll give you a two-thousand-dollar bonus if you'll go down and get your name legally changed." Still, Vida said, "No, sir, I'm sorry. I don't like nicknames or funny names. I like my name just the way it is. It's an unusual name as it is. And it's my father's name."

Finley was not used to being refused. A few days later, while he was warming up to pitch a game, Vida was surprised to see he was listed as True Blue on the message board. He asked the publicity man to have it taken off. When he found out the announcers had been instructed to refer to him as True Blue, he asked them to stop. The more he thought about it the madder he got. He told the story to writers. He asked, "Why doesn't he change his name to True O'Finley?"

This offended Finley, who insists he did not mean it as an insult. He denied he'd offered the youngster more money to change his name than merely enough to cover legal costs. Grumpily he groused, "I think youngsters of today don't understand the old saying, 'true blue.' It means something that is good, something you can count on. I only meant good for him."

By then Finley had signed a black pitcher out of Detroit, Bill Daniels, and announced he had signed "Honey Bear" Daniels, who, he said, was destined to be "the new Vida Blue." When Vida was asked to pose for pictures with "Honey Bear" Daniels, he refused to do so unless he was promised the lad would be referred to as "Bill Daniels" in the captions.

Eventually, Blue even refused to pose for pictures with Finley. Even when Finley asked. When *Sports Illustrated* went to take a photo of Finley with the key players who had produced a run of championships for him, Blue refused to take part in it. When Finley was told, he went to the dressing room and asked Vida himself, and Vida just said, "No." Admiringly, Reggie Jackson says, "A lot of us feel that way about Finley, but few of us have the guts to back it up."

Charles Oscar Finley is a colorful, controversial character, who has turned many on and many more off by the power of his personality. Much has been written about him. Books have been written about him. But it is said that he has not written his own book because he believes it already has been written—"The Bible."

When Jimmy Hunter joined up with Charlie O and became Catfish Hunter, his life, indeed, was changed around. When a player joins up with Charlie O he becomes dominated by him and is altered by the experience. A Jimmy Hunter who was born and reared in a small town to believe in old-fashioned virtues, who believed in loyalty and did not believe in money, wound up suing for his release and auctioning himself off to the highest bidder.

It is said of Charlie O that he is the sort of man who

would like to die in his own arms. And that like all self-made men, he worships his maker.

He *is* a self-made man. He was born near Birmingham, Alabama, in February, 1918. His family lived on a farm. His father and grandfather worked in steel mills. At eighteen Charlie went to work in the mills, too, in Gary, Indiana, where his father had been transferred a few years earlier. It was hard, dirty work, and paid little. Unlike his forebears he was driven to do more with his life.

He worked during the day and went to school and studied at night, attending junior and extension colleges, taking engineering courses. He worked hard and sacrificed a lot of his life to get ahead. When he got married and began a family, he was driven even more. He developed an ulcer which disqualified him from military service during World War II, but he went to work in a defense plant and worked his way up to a position of responsibility. At night he sold insurance.

When the war ended, Finley went to work full time for an insurance company and set a record for policies sold in a single year. But he had driven himself too hard. He developed a persistent cough, which, late in 1946, was diagnosed as an advanced case of pneumonic tuberculosis. He lost half his 200 pounds and almost died before he began to recover. He fought it off. He is a fighter.

He spent more than five months in a sanitorium before he was allowed to leave even for one day, and he spent most of two years there before he was released for good. Recovery was supposed to be a matter of rest, but while he lay in isolation on his back he brooded about his own lack of insurance which had compelled his wife to work to support him. He devised a high-premium, high-payoff accident and illness insurance program that would enable men with a high standard of living to maintain it in the event of illness.

He aimed it at doctors. On his release early in 1948 he went from one insurance company to another in search of one which would underwrite the group program he had devised. Finally, he found the right company. Then he went from one medical group to another trying to sell it. Finally the American College of Surgeons bought it. Then the American Medical Association. Charles O. Finley & Company of Chicago was formed and the proprietor was well on his way to millions. He invested the money that rolled in and made more money. Soon he was wealthy and seeking new worlds to conquer. He had his family at his fancy farm in La Porte, Indiana, a lavish apartment and offices in Chicago, and a lot of free time. He was fascinated by the thought of buying his own baseball team.

As a lad he had become batboy for the Birmingham Barons of the minor league Southern Association. He earned 50 cents and a used baseball each day. (Later, he would buy the ball club.) When he later attended the Indiana University extension school in Gary, his main regret was that he could not afford to study on the main campus in Bloomington so he could go out for the team and play Big Ten ball.

With all his hours of work and study, he found time to play first base for a semipro sandlot team in La Porte evenings and weekends, which he continued until 1946, when he was twenty-eight years old and got sick. Later, when he did buy a big league ball club, he said, "I played semipro ball. If I didn't think I knew something about this game, I wouldn't have made the investment."

During the years between 1948 and 1954 while he was amassing a personal wealth of around $5,000,000 he sponsored semipro and Little League teams, but his ambitions became somewhat higher. In 1954 he bid $3,000,000 for the first team he found for sale, the Philadelphia Athletics, but the team was awarded to Arnold Johnson for the same amount of money and moved to Kansas City in 1955.

Finley offered $5,000,000 for the Detroit Tigers, but they went for more. Then the one he wanted most, the White Sox in his home city of Chicago, went on the block. He bid for them, but they were sold to Bill Veeck. Later, Veeck sold the team, but to his partner, Arthur Allyn, not to Finley.

By then Finley hated the White Sox. But he has bid for them many times since. When an expansion team was awarded to Anaheim, Charlie bid for it, but it was awarded to Gene Autry.

By then the baseball fraternity felt it knew Finley fairly well. He was attending more major league meetings than the men who owned major league teams and he was persistent past the point of reason. He advocated many revolutionary ideas to improve their sport and they resented this outsider trying to tell them what they should do. They could see that if they accepted him into their fraternity, he was the sort who soon would be ruling the frat house. Or trying to. He would be hard to handle. Still, they could not keep him out. His money was not counterfeit. He was clean. His enthusiasm was contagious.

When Arnold Johnson died in 1960, the A's again became available. His widow needed money to pay taxes on her late husband's estate. A group of Kansas City businessmen banded together to purchase stock in the team, but could not come up with the needed money. Finley offered them $2,000,000 for majority interest in the team. In their desperation they accepted his offer. Before long he had bought them out, he had bought the widow out, and for approximately $3,300,000 he had his team.

"There were people who gathered to thank God for Charlie Finley," said one Kansas City businessman. It was not said later.

Finley came in courting the city. He painted the ballpark and installed a scoreboard that exploded into fireworks displays. He virtually painted his players by garbing them in gaudy green and gold uniforms that were ridiculed by the players in more conventional, conservative uniforms. He specialized in special days in which he gave away bats or balls or had his players milking cows or engaging in greased-pig chases. He gave the fans everything except a good team.

He was only forty-three, handsome, charming, and a supersalesman. At his first press conference he announced,

"My intentions are to keep the A's permanently in Kansas City." Through the following months, he announced plans to move his family and settle in the city. He never did. Before long he was trying to transfer the franchise.

He had in the A's contract with the city a clause permitting him to transfer the team if attendance fell below 850,000 in a season. He said this didn't matter. To prove his sincerity, he staged a public ceremony in front of City Hall in which he "burned the contract." It was only later that it turned out he had burned another piece of paper, not the contract.

He sort of liked this stunt. The previous ownership had been under fire from the press and public for having operated a sort of shuttle-bus system to New York, selling or trading many of the A's best ballplayers to the hated Yankees. Finley hated the Yankees more than he hated anyone. When he came in, he publicly burned a bus to symbolize the end of the shuttle run to New York. Shortly thereafter he sent the team's star pitcher, Bud Daley, to the Yankees.

He kept his contract with its controversial clause and when attendance dropped below 850,000 in a season, he started to try to transfer the franchise.

Efforts by city officials to get Finley to sign a new contract proved futile. His lawyers never seemed to be available. "It's only a formality," Charlie insisted. To soothe the city fathers, he placed three of the town's leading citizens on the board of directors of the corporation that ran the team. Only later did it turn out to be a nonexistent corporation. Charlie O ran the team, not any board of directors.

When he took over, he said, "It makes me sick when I read about some owner blaming his team's troubles on the manager." He inherited Joe Gordon as his manager. He said, "He is the best manager in baseball." Three months later he blamed his team's troubles on Gordon and fired the manager. He was only the first. Finley hired and fired managers almost annually. He hired and fired general managers. He made a member of his insurance company the gen-

Russ Reed, Oakland *Tribune*

The pitching form of Catfish Hunter, premustache.

Russ Reed, Oakland *Tribune*

eral manager, then fired him. Finley was his own general manager. And manager. He sent his managers instructions on whom to play and when. "He is never farther away from you than the nearest telephone," said one of his staff. If members of his staff weren't fired, they quit. "We operate with the smallest front office staff in the business," beamed Finley proudly. "To work for me, a man has to be willing to work. If he won't do what I ask of him, I don't want him." One man who worked for him said, "Finley asks more of a man than anyone can give."

The team operated in constant turmoil. When Finley received information that the players had behaved boisterously during some drinking on an airplane flight, he had posted a notice that he deplored the action of players representing the A's and banned drinking on future flights.

The players resentfully drew up their own reply, denying any misbehavior and decrying the use of "informants" on the team. Before releasing it to the press, they showed it to their manager, Alvin Dark. He said it would get him fired, but they were free to do what they wanted. They felt he wouldn't be fired, and released the statement.

Finley was furious and promptly called Dark in to a meeting and fired him. However, as they sat and discussed the team, Dark spoke so glowingly of its potential that Finley rehired him on the spot. While Dark went off to celebrate, Finley went to player representatives to demand they retract their reply. They refused. When they admitted Dark had seen their statement before they had released it, Finley called Dark back in and fired him again.

When the players found out, they were stunned. When writers went to the players for comment, one who would speak was outspoken slugger Ken "the Hawk" Harrelson. He denied the alleged airplane disturbance and criticized Finley for censuring the players.

That evening, a story broke in which Harrelson was quoted as calling Finley "a menace to baseball." Finley angrily reached Harrelson by phone and asked him about his statements. The Hawk said he hadn't called Charlie "a menace," but had said other critical things of Finley. Charlie asked Ken to retract his entire statement. Harrelson refused. Finley fired him.

Someone once said of Finley, "The most predictable thing about Charlie is that he acts unpredictably." Here, he proved it. Instead of trading or selling a valuable player, he simply released him. At first insulted, Harrelson became overjoyed when other clubs began to bid bonuses for him. Chicago called. Then Minnesota. Then Boston. Then Baltimore. Then Atlanta, which offered $100,000. Harrelson asked for $125,000. They settled on $112,000. He accepted. Then Boston called back. They offered $150,000. Harrelson called Atlanta back and asked and received permission to take Boston's better offer. He helped the Red Sox win the pennant too.

It was the only case comparable to Catfish's in recent years, and, of course, it almost had to be Finley who played a prominent part in it. But the money cannot be compared to that offered in the Hunter hunt. However, inflation has set in. Harrelson was not comparable to Hunter as a performer, also; he soon was traded and, dissatisfied, dropped from the game to become a pro golfer but failed at that.

Finley paraded in front of his team a mascot mule he affectionately nicknamed "Charlie O." Finley once was refused permission to parade the mule on another team's field before a game, so he hid him in the clubhouse and brought him on the field during the game. He dressed him in green and gold, traveled him in an air-conditioned trailer, and registered him in the team hotels.

"He treats that mule better than he does some of his players," one of his players griped.

"He is better than some of my players," Finley said laughingly.

He did not have very good players. Under Johnson, the A's usually finished seventh or eighth. Under Finley, they finished ninth or tenth. Attendance dipped below 700,000 fans. He kept saying he would build a good team and keep it in Kansas City, but he kept flying to Dallas, to Oakland, to Louisville, to Milwaukee, to San Diego, to Seattle, to

New Orleans, to Toronto, to Montreal—to any and all towns that at that time did not have a big league team and were willing to talk terms with him.

When Ernie Mehl, the sports editor of the Kansas City *Star*, reported some of this, Finley denied it. Tired of the double-talk, Mehl wrote, "Had the ownership made a deliberate attempt to sabotage a baseball operation, it could not have succeeded as well. There never has been a baseball operation such as this, nothing so bizarre. . . ."

Finley promptly promoted an "Ernie Mehl Appreciation Day" at the ball park, in which he promised to present a "poison pen award" to the writer. Mehl declined to attend, but Finley had the day, during which a truck circled the ball park featuring a characterization of Mehl writing by dipping his pen in a well of poisoned ink. "I thought it was humorous," Finley said. Others did not. Commissioner Ford Frick apologized to the writer on behalf of baseball.

Between denials of his desire to move the team, Finley twice asked the required majority vote of the owners to shift it, once to Dallas and once to Louisville. The owners opposed both moves because there were no satisfactory stadiums in either city and because they were by then opposed to Charlie O on principle alone. By then he had begun to badger them for orange baseballs and "three-ball walks," for designated hitters and designated runners, for games between the teams of the two leagues, for night All-Star and World Series games and so forth.

When they ridiculed him for these, he called them "stupid." He said, "Baseball is back in the dark ages. It's a business, but it is run in a very unbusinesslike manner. If there is one thing I can't stand it's stupidity, and many of my fellow owners are stupid."

So they drew back from him and from his ideas. Many had merit. Eventually they bought some of his schemes. Other teams have adopted more colorful uniforms, exotic scoreboards, and elaborate programs of special promotions. The American League has adopted the designated hitter. The All-Star game and mid-week World Series games now are played at night, when they get tremendous television audiences. But baseball men seldom give Finley credit for revolutionizing their operation.

They didn't want to give him permission to transfer his franchise. When he came up with a city that had a new stadium, Oakland, they refused his request to move there on their first vote. Instead, they asked him to sell his team to Kansas City interests. He refused.

Wrote Ernie Mehl, "If this is major league baseball, we want no part of it." Added his successor, Joe McGuff, "We did not want to get rid of baseball so much as we wanted to get rid of Finley."

Wearily, the owners decided to put a new team into Kansas City, and on their second vote they provided permission for Finley to take his team to Oakland. "Oakland," observed Missouri Senator Stuart Symington, "is the luckiest city since Hiroshima."

After seven disappointing and tumultuous years operating a team in Kansas City, Charles Oscar Finley packed up his team, bats, baggage, and ballplayers, including Catfish Hunter, Reggie Jackson, Sal Bando, and other unknowns who had not as yet done anything to get their names in headlines, and went west.

Staying in Indiana and Chicago, Charlie did not shift a stick of furniture himself, though he rented a luxury apartment high above artificial Lake Merritt in downtown Oakland as his home away from home as an absentee owner who occasionally preferred personal visits to keeping in touch by telephone.

It was 1968 and he was fifty, but he looked a little older. His good looks had gone to gray hair and a flushed face. And life in Oakland would take a little more out of him, hitting him with a couple of heart attacks. But he'd bounce back, as flamboyant as ever, pushed through hotel lobbies in a wheelchair, cheered by celebrating fans at World Series time, having his pulse taken by his personal physician who sat by his side in his flag-draped boxes after his team hit the top.

"Nothing changes Charlie. He changes you, but you can't change him," Catfish Hunter has been heard to say.

6

Oakland welcomed Finley and his players with closed arms. He signed a long-term contract to play there in order to get attractive terms for his stay and almost before the ink was dry he was beginning to look for other towns that might offer him better terms and for ways to break his pact with the city.

Although this area of northern California is considered to have a population of around 5,000,000, they are spread out over fifty miles or more. Oakland itself has only 365,000. San Francisco, across the bay, has only 725,000.

San Francisco is considered a town of sophisticates; Oakland a town of working people. San Franciscans seldom cross the bay to visit Oakland. Oaklanders resent this. The rivalry is real between these sister cities, who would spill one another's blood on the water between them.

San Francisco already had a team, the Giants. They had lost interest in the Giants, so the fans there weren't interested in the new team, the A's, across the Bay. Nor were the hard hats in Oakland turned on by the new team. The A's attendance did go up in Oakland, while the Giants' went down in San Francisco, but most years neither drew a million, the Giants went down near a half-million, and there were years when together they drew just about what the one had drawn before.

The Bay Area didn't give Finley much more than Kansas City had. And actually he gave Oakland one thing he had not given Kansas City—a good team. He threw in all the other stuff—the fireworks and fan appreciation days—but the fans didn't appreciate him and his, so he started to cancel their special days.

When the team turned into a champion and still wasn't supported in the style it deserved, he became embittered and began to fish around again for new waters in which to locate his floating ballgame. Seattle? Toronto? New Orleans? "We're unappreciated here," he growled in that voice of his, deep as the devil's must be.

How about sending the White Sox to Seattle and giving him and his A's his hometown of Chicago? The owners opposed him at every turn, but he had broken their resistance before and he thought he could again. They suggested he sell, instead, as they had in Kansas City. His doctors wanted him to sell, too. "Maybe," he growled, but he didn't.

His wife separated from him, hired protection from him, sued for divorce from him, sued for nonsupport by him. His insurance business reportedly had lost key clients and was struggling, though he denied it. His hockey and basketball teams had been neglected onto the brink of bankruptcy before he forced their leagues to buy them back from him to save them. Sell his baseball team? What, then, would be left in his life?

"I built the best ball club in history by myself," he growled, neglecting the players with which he built it. "It is my life," he growled, neglecting the lives he altered in the running of it.

In Kansas City he built the base for the winner which built up in Oakland. At a time before the big league draft of available amateurs went into effect, when the top prospects could be turned pro by any team which could talk them into it, he bought Catfish Hunter, Reggie Jackson, Sal Bando, Blue Moon Odom, Rick Monday, and others for big bonuses. They were developing in Kansas City. They developed in Oakland.

He had to pay a lot to get some of them, but once he had them he did not have to pay a lot to keep them. "When they bargain for big salaries, they forget their big bonuses," he growled. He didn't growl when he got them. A supersalesman from the day he won a bike with a record run of magazine subscriptions obtained door to door, he charmed youngsters he wanted and persuaded their parents he would be like a father to them.

"My players are like my sons," he has said.

Catfish Hunter's eyes still get big when he recalls the green and gold caps and bats Charlie handed out when he descended on Hertford, North Carolina. Blue Moon Odom blinks with awe as he remembers Charlie pulling up in front of his humble Macon, Georgia, home with a rented half-ton truck full of vegetables, chickens, and other food, which he then passed on to the parents. It was graduation night and the lad signed that night.

"What other owner would go where I've gone to get players? Who would do what I do?" asks Charlie O.

He invested in a scouting system that tipped him to the potential of a Campy Campaneris, a Claudell Washington, and a Vida Blue, who went overlooked by others and thus could be bought cheap. Actually a shrewd judge of talent, he authorized deals that brought in a Kenny Holtzman, Darold Knowles, Billy North, and others who have helped him win.

He did not like losing. Who does? When Hank Bauer, who had been hired and fired as manager in Kansas City, was hired again as manager in Oakland and failed to win with the A's, he was again fired. John McNamara was hired and fired as manager. Dick Williams became the eleventh manager of the A's in eleven years and he won with the team, so he stayed a while.

Williams inherited players who were getting good enough to win and he taught them how to win. He taught them to execute properly the fundamental plays that win games. He showed them the number of hits they get are not as important as when they get the hits. He showed them the hit the pitcher gives up can be counterbalanced by the hit the fielders take away.

Maybe the most important thing he taught them was how to live with their owner. Live and let live was his policy. Let Finley do what he wanted, their job was to do what they could do. He refused to fight with Finley, but he taught his players to fight. They fought their foes, they fought Finley, they even fought among themselves, but they performed on the field. They won, so what did it matter?

Finley popped off, so he couldn't deny them the right to pop off. Once they found out they could get away with it, it became a way of life for them. As long as they won, what difference did it make? As long as they won, Finley could care less. After Finley offered them money to grow mustaches for a special day, they refused to shave them off. They let their hair grow. And they won. They became as proud of their performance as of their image. Their pride prodded them.

They won the divisional title in 1971, but lost the pennant play-off. The next year they won not only the divisional title and the pennant play-off, but the World Series as well. The next year they repeated. And in 1974 they made it three in a row, an accomplishment surpassed only by the old Yankees. A brawling, bearded bunch, the Angry A's had become the dominant team in baseball.

They overcame all obstacles. When Dick Williams resigned after the 1974 season, finally fed up with Finley, Charlie O wished him well wherever he would go. But when Williams sought to sign with the Yankees, Finley refused him permission, branded him as bound by his contract, and signed as a substitute Alvin Dark to his second term as manager of the A's.

Dark had been out of baseball awhile and was unsure of himself. Finley managed for him, which made him look foolish. The players were angered by him and ridiculed him. But eventually he earned their grudging respect and they won with him.

Meanwhile, when the Angels sought Williams, Finley finally released him. After all, they were a losing team. When Williams returned to Oakland with the Angels, and lost to the A's Finley saluted him on the scoreboard—WEL-COME BACK.

"He may have millions," observed Bob Elson, one of Finley's former broadcasters, "but he doesn't have a nickel's worth of class."

Aside from a single loyalist, Monte Moore, Finley's radio and TV announcers have come and gone about as fast as his managers. He had 15 in 14 years. One of them, Red Rush, observes, "He'd keep calling up to tell his announcers we were saying too much about baseball and not enough about Charlie Finley." Another, Jim Woods, says, "When he fired me he said I didn't make the games exciting enough when nothing was going on."

He is always warring with the writers, who are not in his employ. When they displeased him, he cut their free dinners at the ball park to the first 50. He has cut the pass list to the bone. He has barred some from the ballpark or removed them from the traveling parties.

Ron Bergman of the Oakland *Tribune,* the only reporter who regularly travels with the team, reports, "He constantly calls up to complain about bad stories. But when you try to call him, he's not in." Wells Twombly of the San Francisco *Examiner* says, "He can be trying to charm you one minute and trying to cut your throat the next."

But of all the people he has alienated, the players have to head up the list. Many admire his ability, but few respect his performance.

Bound into bondage by their contract, the slaves of the sporting world resent their masters. When one is as heavy-handed as Finley is, manipulating them like pawns in his private game, he is hated. They are compensated by cash, but no amount of money can make them like the sort of life they lead under the ownership of a Charlie O.

Reggie Jackson, one of the richest of the rebels, says he asked $100,000 when he signed and was given $95,000. He says, "I figured Finley out. He is never going to give you what you want."

His second season, his salary was $20,000. He made a run at Ruth's homer record for a while and wound up with 47 home runs. He asked for $60,000. Finley offered $40,000. Reggie held out until spring training was almost over.

Russ Reed, Oakland *Tribune*

Talking it over during a tough moment on the mound with Sal
Bando, left, manager Dick Williams, center, and catcher Dave
Duncan, right.

Afraid the season would get away from him, he signed for the forty.

He was bitter about it. Maybe he was right, maybe he was wrong, but he was bitter. He was young and he felt Finley had cheated him. For the first time he realized that in baseball you play for what your owner will pay you or you don't play.

He had a bad season and Finley ordered him benched. Finley tried to talk Reggie into going to the minors voluntarily and Reggie refused. When he hit a home run in front of Finley, he stopped at home plate and saluted the owner with an obscene gesture. Threatening him with a fine or suspension, Finley talked Reggie into making an announcement of apology. The player felt humiliated.

The pressure the player had felt from the press and public when he was going well was compounded by the pressure he felt from Finley when he was going badly. He said, "Baseball was not for me what I expected it to be." He said, "An owner like Finley puts it to you whenever he wants to. It's legalized rape."

He said, "I got to where I didn't want any more big years. I got to where I just wanted to have good years, help my team win, and get a little raise every year without anyone noticing me."

He had a couple of years like that. But he was driven to do better. He said, "I decided I was cheating myself, my family, my friends, my teammates, the fans, and even my owner if I didn't make the most of what I had in me."

He put it all together in 1973. He drove in 117 runs, led the A's to the divisional title, was unanimously voted Most Valuable Player in the league, and when he helped his side win the World Series, too, was voted MVP of that, too.

Confident now, proud of his position in his sport, he stood up to the fans, to the writers, and to Finley. By then he was making $75,000 a season and he asked a raise to $135,000. Finley offered $100,000. Reggie took him to arbitration and the board voted in favor of the player.

More A's went to arbitration than any other team and

Finley lost more cases than any other owner. Reggie shrugged and said, "If we have to fight for our rights, we'll fight. We win, not Finley." He no longer was afraid of Finley. He even enjoyed him at times now. "He's a good old dude at times," Jackson says with a shrug.

But the bygone bitternesses between them stuck to him like a stain. He remembered his rookie year, when he jammed his thumb. Before the following game, the team physician, Dr. Harry Walker, told the writers Reggie's injury was such he could not play for a few days.

But between then and the game, Finley talked to the doctor and it was decided Reggie could play. Told he was going to play, Reggie was angered. When the doctor examined him after the game, Reggie grabbed a scalpel out of his doctor's bag and slashed the bandage off his thumb so savagely he sliced his thumb. If he wasn't hurt, he said, he didn't need a bandage.

When the writers asked the doctor why he had permitted Jackson to play, the doctor said he had decided the player hadn't been hurt as badly as he at first had believed. Reggie says, "Since then I've been asked to play many times when I was hurt. I think there is a difference between team doctors and doctors. I think the team wants to win so much they don't care about the player."

There have been several such incidents on Charlie O's Angry A's.

The incident that stands out was the one in the World Series of 1973 when Mike Andrews was asked to play second base despite a shoulder injury and made two errors that contributed to the A's loss in the second game.

Afterward an angry Finley met with the doctor and Andrews in a private session that produced a letter of resignation from the player, saying his shoulder was too sore for him to play properly and he was leaving the team. Presumably this would permit Finley to add to the team a player he had been denied permission to add earlier.

However, when the writers got to Andrews, he said he had been pressured into saying something that was not true. The players angrily spoke in his defense, threatening to strike. Commissioner Bowie Kuhn ordered the player reinstated, heaping fuel on the fire that already raged between him and an embarrassed Finley.

Later, Finley was fined by Kuhn for this and other irregular acts, but it did not alter the owner. Later, Dick Williams said this was the straw that broke the back of his business setup with the owner and finally persuaded him to resign from Finley, though it meant he was leaving a championship club.

"If you can get away from that man, you get away," said Vida Blue with a sigh, echoing the same sort of sentiments confessed by Catfish Hunter a year or so later.

Blue was bitter from the moment Charlie O tried to get him to change his name. Like Reggie, he was disenchanted by what happened to his life when he became a big man in baseball. "You become a trophy, not a man," he said with a sigh. Like Reggie, he was disenchanted by his failure to get the sort of salary from Finley the player thought he had earned.

Following his first full season when he won 25 games and the Cy Young Award as the American League's top pitcher, Blue asked through an attorney for $115,000 and Finley offered $50,000. This was before the beginning of arbitration, and when neither would give in there was no one to settle the issue.

Blue held out until the season had started and then gave in when Finley upped his offer to $63,000. After signing he said, "Charlie Finley has soured my stomach for baseball. He treated me like a damn colored boy. All I wanted was to be treated like a man."

He was behind in his conditioning and he had a bad season. He came back to win 20 the next season, but he no longer looked like the pitcher he had been in the beginning. Jackson says, "He could be better, he could care less now. He has no enthusiasm for it. He turns it on only when he wants."

Vida grins, putting people on. "Hey, man, I just throw the

ball. They hit it or they don't. Nothing I can do about it. I play the game and I pick up my pay. Just doing a job. It's not a game, it's a job. I play my games away from the ball park. Charlie? I don't think about him. I don't think anything about him."

When Catfish escaped, Vida said, "Good for him."

When Vida was hot, Finley had him saved for the big-gate games, even if it meant moving Hunter in and out of the rotation. Hunter hated it. He was on his way to 20 victories for the first time, too. But he wasn't big at the box office and Blue was. "I don't like it, but I understand. It's not easy to take, but I have to take it," the Cat commented.

When Vida was hot, Finley held a "day" in his honor to drum up added business. Among other things he gave Blue a blue car. It made a good picture and a good story and it made Charlie look good. Until later when it turned out he had given the player the car, but not ownership of the car.

"When Mr. Finley gives you something, you should look for the strings on it," Blue said laughingly.

Over the years Charles O. Finley has given Jim "Catfish" Hunter quite a bit, but a lot of it came with strings attached. Aside from his original bonus, there was a $5,000 bonus for him when he pitched a perfect game in 1968, but that was tacked onto his salary when he sought a raise the following season.

Aside from recommending an investment in 1972 which netted Hunter $15,000 after taxes, there was a loan of $150,000 in 1970 to buy almost 500 acres of farmland, but that turned sour when Finley insisted on repayment ahead of schedule so he could buy a hockey team, the California Seals, and a basketball team, the Memphis Pros, both of which went sour, with poor attendance.

It was during contract talks prior to Hunter's sixth season with the A's that he mentioned one reason he wanted a raise was to buy a 485-acre farm in his neighborhood, on which he could build a home, plant crops, raise cattle, and live the sort of life he wanted to live the rest of his life. As long as he was playing, this life and the hunting walks through the woods would keep his legs in shape and keep him in shape.

Finley conceded that it sounded like a good investment. "What do you need?" he asked.

"One hundred and fifty thousand dollars," Hunter said.

"No problem," Finley said.

"I don't know when I can pay you back," Hunter said.

"Don't worry about it. It's no problem," Finley said.

The next day the owner wrote Hunter a check for $150,000.

"When he first lent me the money," recalls Catfish, "we had a verbal agreement, never anything written down. He sent the money straight into my bank under my name. He didn't have any attachments to it. But it was understood it was a loan.

"We worked out an agreement that I was to pay him back at least twenty thousand dollars a year at the end of every baseball season with six percent interest until it was paid off.

"I appreciated that loan. I really wanted that land. I knew I could pay back the money every year with the kind of money I was making.

"But then, three or four months into the season, Finley started asking me to pay the money back.

"He'd say, 'Jim, you owe me one hundred fifty thousand dollars and I've got to have it. I need it because I'm buying basketball and hockey teams.'

"And I'd say, 'But, Mr. Finley, you said I could pay it off twenty thousand dollars a year.'

"And he'd just say, 'Well, I'm sorry, but I need it now.'

"He'd call me in the clubhouse. He'd call me off the field. He called me at the hotels on the road. He called me at home. He called my father, who was furious.

"I tried to arrange loans in Oakland and by telephone to North Carolina, but I couldn't.

"I'd ask him, 'How can I pay you back during the season? Let me go home between starts and make arrangements for the money.' But he'd say, 'No, you can't. You've got to stay and pitch.'

"But in August when it was the worst he called me every day I was due to pitch. He didn't call me on the other days, just the days I was due to pitch.

"I asked him once why he only called me on the days I was due to pitch, but he said he didn't know when I was going to pitch.

"That was a bunch of bull because Charlie knows everything that's going on in this club. He tells the managers who to pitch and when.

"I tried not to think the worst of him, but it was impossible. I was having my best year, but he hurt it badly. His calls upset me so much I didn't win a single one of my seven starts in August.

"I won eighteen games that year. I should have won twenty for the first time. It's the last time I didn't win twenty. But going without a win that entire month cost me my twenty.

"Finally I was so desperate I went to Finley and said, 'Give me one hundred fifty thousand tax free and I'll sign a contract that won't cost you another cent for years.'

"It would have been stupid on my part, but he was so stubborn he didn't see the sense of it and refused it. He would have been getting a big bargain.

"Finally the season ended and I went home and tried to get a loan to cover it, but the boundary line was in dispute so I couldn't get it. He was still calling so I just said the hell with it and I sold four fifths of the farm for $150,000 and sent him his money back.

"I paid him that damn loan six months after I got it and had to pay $6,000 in interest to boot, but later he did refund the interest.

"We were just cheap farmers, that's all we ever were. If I had the full farm today, it would be worth three-to-four-hundred thousand, maybe five hundred thousand. But I did come out 100 acres or so ahead.

"Still, that's when I made up my mind that I couldn't trust him. From then on I made sure I got everything he said down on paper."

Accordingly, Catfish's contract for 1974 had in it the clause that half his salary was to be paid into an investment program for him. When Finley did not, the courts upheld the contract.

Although the story was known to insiders and rumors of it had spread outside the team, Catfish refused to confirm it until Charlie referred to the loan as an example of his generosity.

He did so when Hunter and other A's complained about Charlie's "cheap" championship rings provided the players as per custom after their 1973 World Series win. He did so again when Hunter took him to court to obtain his release.

Then Hunter spoke openly of the loan and how it worked out.

"Mr. Finley often does go out of his way to be nice to ballplayers. He's been nice to a lot of us. He's helped us make some good investments and he's made us loans. He paid some of us big bonuses to sign, but he is a tough man at contract time," Hunter admits. "But I was bitter about the way he called in the loan. My father still is. He mishandled my contract in 1974. And I've seen him mistreat a lot of players. And managers. And other employees. He'll do a good thing and then spoil it by doing a bad thing.

"When Mr. Finley thinks he can treat you like an animal, he'll do it. That's when you know it's time to leave.

"He had put together one of the great teams of all time. I was proud to be a part of it. I hated to leave it. I'd spent ten years with him and his team. I became a top pitcher with him and his team. But the time had come to leave. And I could live with leaving him. I have some bad memories of my time with him. I have some good memories of my time with the team, however."

7

On the eighth of May, 1968, early in his fourth season with the A's and his first in Oakland, Catfish Hunter faced the Minnesota Twins in the cement saucer called the Coliseum. He had just turned twenty-two years of age, he had won only 30 games in three prior years in the majors, and he had lost more games than he had won. Nothing special was expected of him, but as the night game went on the excitement increased until the small crowd was shouting with every pitch.

Hunter threw only 107 pitches during the game and he had almost complete control of each of them. He threw 55 strikes, 38 called balls, and 16 pitches that were hit into outs. He struck out 11 batters and did not walk a one. And his teammates played errorlessly in the field behind him. It was a perfect performance.

"I threw only three change-ups and only one curve all night," Hunter reported later. "I started out throwing mostly fastballs and sliders and when I saw they were working I made up my mind to go with those pitches. There were four that were hit hard, but only one that worried me."

In the fourth inning, Cesar Tovar hit a pitch on a line to left, but it was right at Joe Rudi, who was making his first start since arriving from Vancouver that day, and the rookie caught it.

In the fifth inning, Ted Uhlaender drove a pitch deep to right, but Reggie Jackson hauled it in.

The next batter, Bob Allison, blasted a grounder hard right at third baseman Sal Bando. It took a high hop, but Bando grabbed it and fired to first for the out.

In the seventh, Rod Carew ripped a drive to left, but Rudi angled back on it, got to it just in time, got his glove on it, and hung onto it.

That was the one that worried Hunter. "I thought it might get by Rudi," Catfish said later.

It worried the rookie, too. "I was hoping the ball wouldn't be hit to me, I was so nervous," Rudi admitted later. "When it was, I thought it was over my head. But I got back in time to get it."

That was the second out of the inning and everyone was nervous by then, for Hunter had not permitted a batter to reach base. The next batter was Harmon Killebrew. The count went to 3 and 2. Hunter threw one of his change-ups. An off-speed slider. "The greatest and guttiest pitch of the game," manager Bob Kennedy commented. "The Killer" swung so hard and missed by so much that the bat flew out of his hands and headed right for Hunter, who ducked. The bat sailed harmlessly into the grass at second base after almost decapitating the pitcher.

"That made me as nervous as anything," Catfish conceded later. "I was more worried about him than anyone else all game, anyway."

"Why me?" Harmon asked later. "He struck me out three times. Twice he fooled me and I took the third strikes. He had me off balance."

"Well," said Hunter, "he was the best bet to break up the ball game with one swing of the bat and it was so close I was as worried about being beaten as I was about getting a no-hitter most of the way."

In fact, it was still scoreless in the last of the seventh when his teammates, who superstitiously refused to talk about the no-hitter all night, started to tease Hunter about being taken out for a pinch hitter.

Dave Boswell had blanked the A's on five hits until Rick Monday doubled to center to start the seventh. After Rudi struck out, the possibility of a pinch hitter for the pitcher came up.

"I never considered it," A's manager Kennedy said later. "Catfish can handle the bat too well."

He had, in fact, gotten one of the earlier hits, a double before being stranded in the third.

Now he was sent up to hit. A hit would snap the scoreless deadlock. A wild pitch by Boswell had sent Monday to third base.

Hunter was sent the signal to bunt in an effort to squeeze the runner home.

He bunted down the third-base line. He laid it on the ground so gently, the fielders had no play as Monday hustled home and Hunter raced to first for a single.

Campy Campaneris then popped out and Reggie Jackson was called out on strikes, but the Catfish returned to the mound for the eighth inning having staked himself to a 1–0 lead.

Tony Oliva, a two-time batting champion who would later win a third title, was first up and dangerous, but Hunter retired him on a pop-up. Uhlaender stroked a soft fly to Rudi in left. Veteran Bob Allison bounced a grounder that Campaneris handled cleanly and fired to first for the out.

The fans stood and cheered the Catfish back to the dugout.

In the home half, the A's padded the margin. Bando and Ramon Webster stroked singles. John Donaldson and Jim Pagliaroni hit into force-outs. But Monday was walked. When Boswell threw two called balls to pinch hitter Floyd Robinson, Ron Perranoski relieved. Danny Cater pinch-hit for the pinch hitter and was walked, forcing in a run.

Hunter then singled for his third hit and second and third runs batted in of the ball game. By the time Campaneris grounded into a force-out at second, Hunter had a 4–0 lead.

Now, the ninth, the fans hollering on every pitch. Veteran John Roseboro pinch-hit and grounded out to John Donaldson to cheers. Bruce Look came up and was called out on strikes to more cheers.

Finally, young Rich Reese pinch-hitting. The tension was terrific. "I was sweating. I was scared to death," Catfish admitted later.

Working carefully, he went to 2 and 2 on the batter. At this point he knew he had a perfect game. He not only wanted the no-hitter, he did not want to walk anyone.

Four more times he threw to Reese. Four times the hitter fouled the pitches back. With each pitch, each swing, and each foul, the crowd groaned and the tension increased.

Hunter fired a fastball for the inside part of the plate and the batter took it. Catcher Pagliaroni raised a triumphant fist and started to run for the mound, but the umpire barked, "Ball three!"

Pagliaroni pivoted and started to argue with the umpire, Larry Neudecker. Later, the catcher confessed, "I was prejudiced when I complained. But in that situation I thought we'd get the call.

"He called a fine game. That was a borderline call."

"It was inside," the umpire reported later.

"It was a foot inside," Reese said.

The Catfish stalked around the mound, scuffling his foot in the dirt until the argument abated. He wanted to keep his concentration. The noise in the arena pounded down on him.

Gathering himself, Hunter rared back and fired a fastball, high. Reese ripped at it and missed it.

Hunter gave a little jump of joy on the mound as the catcher came out of his crouch on the dead run for him. Their entire team erupted out of the dugout or came from their field positions to congratulate him.

With the missed swing, the fans exploded in a roar and they continued clapping and hollering, all standing now, as the A's pulled a protesting Hunter up on their shoulders and carried him a few feet before he squirmed off and ran off.

"I was embarrassed," he admitted happily, later.

It was the first perfect game pitched during a regular season in the American League in 46 years, since Charlie Robertson had hurled one in 1922. Sandy Koufax had thrown one in the National League in 1965. And Don Larson had thrown one for the American League Yankees against the National League Dodgers in 1956.

But, they were rare. Only 12 had been tossed in the history of baseball and five of these had come when baseball was a different game, before the turn of the century. Jim Bunning, Koufax, Larsen, and Hunter had the only ones in more than 50 years by 1975.

That night in 1968 Catfish's spectacular performance was almost totally unexpected. He was a youngster trying to find his form, he was not an established star, and he never would be the sort of pitcher to overpower the opposition as, say, a Koufax could.

But he showed the signs of things to come.

Charlie Finley's favorite saying is, "The Three S's— Sweat Plus Sacrifice Equals Success." The players are sick of hearing it. They make fun of it. But there is truth to it. Catfish Hunter concedes, "Success didn't come easy to me. I had to sweat for it. I had to sacrifice for it."

It took five or six seasons for him to put his talent together.

Signed as an eighteen-year-old in the summer of 1964, he was assigned to Daytona Beach in the Florida State League, but never actually was sent there. He still was recovering from the second surgery on his right foot. "I didn't do anything except pitch batting practice," he recalls.

Because of the "bonus baby" rule then in effect in baseball, in which players who received more than $4,000 to sign had to spend their first full season in the majors, Hunter, recovered, went right to the A's in Kansas City in 1965.

Carried by their clubs, few of these bonus babies played. Plans called for Catfish to watch from the bench in 1965, then be sent for seasoning to the minors the following season. The way it worked out, he never has pitched an inning in the minors.

"I got what they call a lazy arm from pitching batting practice the last half of the 1964 season," Hunter recalls.

"We had sluggers like Rocky Colavito and Jim Gentile on the club then and I just laid the ball in to them.

"That winter I went to the Instructional League to get some work. There were a few top prospects on teams there, but not many. I had a no-hitter, but it was just one of those games when everything went my way. I won five or six games and lost five or six.

"A scout told me I had a lazy arm. I wasn't snapping the ball. I also still was sidearming a lot. In my senior year in high school a couple of the scouts told me I'd better start throwing overhand or I'd never make it, and I worked on it. But after my layoff I fell back into bad habits. I was stubborn.

"I threw a lot of strikes. But they hit a lot of them, too. I wasn't throwing as hard as I had in high school and I didn't know how to compensate for it. I threw too many slow curves. I could put the pitches where I wanted, but I didn't know where to put them.

"I hadn't learned the batters. I didn't know how to work on them, how to set them up to make them hit the pitch I wanted them to hit. I hadn't learned how to concentrate. I let my mind wander a lot. I let everything that went wrong bother me.

"Moe Drabowsky was there then and he helped me more than anything, but I needed a lot of help.

"I had good stuff, but I had as many bad games as good games.

"In the spring of 1965, Clyde Kluttz said I wasn't throwing hard enough, but I didn't do much about it until a story about me in *The Sporting News*. The headline said, THROW THE CATFISH BACK. I got mad at myself. I started working harder. I had to work to get back what I had lost in my year off."

The A's were not a good team at that time, but they had no thought of using young Hunter. With a 57–105 record they had finished tenth in 1964. Ed Lopat had been replaced as manager at midseason by Mel McGaha. With a 59–103 record, they finished tenth again in 1965 and

McGaha was replaced as manager early in the season by Haywood Sullivan.

The only regulars on that team who remained regulars later when the team reached the top were the double-play combination of Dick Green and Bert Campaneris. "Hawk" Harrelson was the first baseman, but he hit only .232. No one hit .300. Or even .290. Or .280. Harrelson provided the only power with 23 home runs. He only drove in 66 runs, but that was the best on the team.

Other regulars such as Ed Charles, Mike Hershberger, Jim Landis, Tommy Reynolds, and Bill Bryan hardly are remembered today.

Nor were the pitchers memorable. The top starters were Fred Talbot and Rollie Sheldon. They won only 10 games each, and together they lost as many as they won. John O'Donoghue won 9, but lost twice as many as he won. Eventually this mediocrity provided an opportunity for the nineteen-year-old Hunter to break in.

He debuted as a pro on the thirteenth of May against the White Sox in Chicago. Working in relief, he pitched two innings in which he did not give up a hit or a run. He returned against the White Sox less than a week later and gave up only one run over the first three innings he worked, but then was bombed out.

Hunter came on again in Minnesota against the Twins. He took over in the second inning with the bases loaded and one out. He bailed his side out with a double-play pitch. He retired the side in order in the third. He loaded the bases in the fourth on a walk and two cheap hits, but worked his way out of the jam.

When he walked the first batter to face him the following inning, manager Sullivan went out to take him out. He told him, "Catfish, you can pitch the rest of your life and you won't get in any more trouble than you've been in tonight. I'm taking you out before something else happens."

Sullivan recalled, "His only reaction was a big grin."

Sullivan said, "I decided to use him in long relief before giving him his first start. He was extremely inexperienced and I wanted to give him the feel of things before throwing him to the wolves. I hoped he'd do well enough to gain confidence in himself."

Pitching coach Tom Feerick said, "Hunter has unusual poise and control for a pitcher with his lack of experience. He'll need that control to be a consistent winner. He's not an overpowering type of pitcher. He has good stuff, but he'll have to try to pitch like a man of twenty-five or twenty-six to win consistently."

It was prophetic because Catfish was twenty-four before he won more games than he lost, and twenty-five before he won 20 games in a season.

It was July before Hunter was given his first start. "The season was more than half over before I was taken out of the bullpen," Hunter recalls. "The only reason I got to start was our fifth starter, Don Buschorn, came up with a sore arm.

"They didn't have any other starters for spot starts, so they tried me. I did well enough so they just forgot about him. That was the only year he ever pitched in the majors. And I did well enough so they forget about sending me out to the minors the next season.

"My first start was in July in the second game of a double-header with Detroit. We got seven runs in the first inning, so I should have breezed, but I couldn't get through the second inning. I was taken out after I gave up two runs and put two men on base. We turned around and lost the game.

"My first victory was on the twenty-seventh of the month in Boston and I wasn't too impressive. We won, ten to eight. I went five innings. Three relief pitchers saved it. Jim Lonborg lost it. That was my second start. But they started me fairly regularly after that and I did better after that. I had some bad games, but I had some good games, too."

He hurled two shutouts. He blanked Boston, 8–0, on only two hits, and Detroit, 5–0, on six hits. He also beat the Yankees in Yankee Stadium, 4–1, on four hits, walking only two. An early home run by Roger Repoz deprived him of his shutout.

Proof that he was bombed at times is shown in his high earned-run average of 4.36 per game. He completed only 3 of 20 starts. He won 8 decisions and lost 8. But he impressed his bosses with his potential and his "Yes, sir" and "No, sir" manners.

"He is a young man who has had the right upbringing," observed Charlie O. "He has a good attitude and a lot of ability. I believe he will become a star for our team and be a good example for the young men of Kansas City."

A's executive vice-president Eddie Lopat, the former star pitcher, said, "He has a chance to be a great pitcher. He has more aptitude for pitching than anyone I've ever seen at his age. He has natural ability and determination. He has the right temperament for a pitcher. He's smart. He stays cool and tries to learn."

He was sent to play winter ball in Venezuela to learn more about his trade. "I learned that's not my kind of life," he recalled later, laughing.

"The fans are wild. They're always singing, dancing, or fighting in the stands. They scare you when you do badly and they get on you. One night the umpire made a bad call and the fans got on him. He turned to the stands and pulled out a revolver. That ended the noise. After that I was afraid of the umpires, too.

"Prices were high. I lived with Paul Lindblad, Lew Krausse, and Rene Lachmemann and we paid four hundred dollars for our apartment. We sent one of their own, Jose Tartabull, to bargain for us and they still got us for four hundred dollars. We did most of our own cooking. I lost weight. I couldn't drink the water or eat the food without getting sick. It's pretty country, but I didn't have much time to enjoy it.

"I was starting one day and relieving the next. My arm got sore. I told our manager. He told me to go out and try some more. When I'm asked to work, I give it all I've got.

My arm got to hurting pretty bad. I asked the manager to call Lopat, but he didn't. I finally called Lopat and he said, 'Get home, Catfish.' I got home. It was cold and snowing in North Carolina, but I was so happy to be home I didn't care. I laid off pitching for a while and my arm recovered."

A 6-foot, 185-pounder when he reported originally, Hunter had put on weight. In spring training in Florida prior to the 1966 season, he suffered shin splints while running in an effort to reduce. "I couldn't run. Nobody thought I was in shape and I wasn't."

Given the honor of hurling the opening game, he performed impressively, though beaten, 2–1, in Minnesota. However, he lost his first three before he began to win. Then he was surprised by being selected for the All-Star Game at midseason in St. Louis.

"It caught me by surprise," he confessed. "I didn't think I would ever make it, and I mean *ever*. And I probably wouldn't have made it this time if they didn't have to pick somebody from every team.

"They should have picked our relief pitcher, Jack Aker. He's been our best, but he hasn't been at his best against Minnesota, and the Minnesota manager, Sam Mele, made the selections because he's the All-Star manager.

"I've been erratic. I'm throwing harder than I was last season, but when I throw too hard I get wild, and control is my game. I know the batters better this season than I did last season, but when I feel strong I try to overpower them instead of pitching to their weaknesses.

"People say to me, 'You can win fifteen easy this year.' That's right. But I also can lose fifteen, and that's not right."

He not only pitched in the All-Star Game, but he pitched more than anyone else. That's because the pitcher who goes into extra innings is not limited to three innings as are the others. Hunter pitched four shutout innings before being beaten by the fourth hit off him in his fifth inning, the fifteenth of the game, when Tony Perez hit a home run to give the National League the victory.

Russ Reed, Oakland *Tribune*

Young Jim Hunter doffs his cap following a triumph.

The perfect-game pitcher and his wife, Helen, show off souvenir ball from his 1968 no-hit masterpiece against the Minnesota Twins.

Shortly thereafter the Catfish was stricken with appendicitis and had to have an emergency operation in Boston. He was feeling bad on Sunday night, but after the team flew into Boston on Monday he felt better. He went out to eat with roomate Lew Krausse that night and started to feel bad again. He vomited, threw up blood, and was rushed to Santa Maria Hospital to have his appendix removed.

His record was 9–9 at the time and he was out two months. He came back just before season's end to lose two starts, closing out his curtailed campaign with a 9–11 record and a 4.02 ERA. He had pitched only 4 complete games in 30 starts. Clearly, despite some high points, it was a disappointing season. He had ballooned to 205 pounds and Finley was disappointed in him. There was a lot of talk of trading him.

Still, he was only twenty years old and would not be twenty-one until the next season started. He went home determined to work himself back into shape.

On the tenth of October he got married. "That didn't help. Helen's too good a cook. And I like to eat. Weight is one of my big battles." He smiled. "But it settled me down. I worked on my brother's farm. I ran a bulldozer every day.

"Every Sunday when the weather was good I worked out at the ball park there with my brothers. Before I went south for spring training, I started working out with the kids in high school. I did a lot of walking in the woods, hunting. I got down to one-hundred-ninety-five pounds and I got my legs strong. When the season started, I was ready."

It was a tumultuous season, the last for the A's in Kansas City.

Under new manager Alvin Dark they had soared to seventh place with a 74–86 mark in 1966. Lew Krausse and Jim Nash had joined with Catfish Hunter in giving the team promising young pitchers and there were some promising young hitters moving up.

However, the team sagged back into the cellar with a 62–99 record in 1967 as Dark and Harrelson were fired in the celebrated controversy which centered on Krausse's alleged airflight misconduct in which he supposedly harassed a stewardess. Rick Monday, Reggie Jackson, and Sal Bando broke in, but Krausse and Nash came apart.

Hunter hurled himself right off the trading block. He won only 13 games and lost 17, but most observers thought he should have turned that record around. He wasn't given a run in 6 of his starts and only 1 run in 4 others, so there were 10 he could have won. He finished 13 of 35 starts, worked 260 innings, and had an impressive ERA of 2.80.

Luke Appling completed the campaign as manager and commented, "Hunter has made a lot of progress. He's not there yet, but he's getting there, and he will get there. It takes time for a pitcher like he is. He's a youngster who works like a veteran. The more he learns, the better he'll be, and he's learning."

Hunter says, "I learned a lot under Dark and really was sorry to see him go. You could talk to him and he got you to trying different things. Appling was a lame-duck manager. It wasn't his fault, but we knew we were leaving town and would get a new manager when we got to our new town.

"Finley had become very unpopular in Kansas City and they took it out on the team. There were rumors always flying around and it made it hard to keep your mind on your business. Moving was unsettling."

Bob Kennedy became the manager in Oakland. Before Hunter's start at home on the eighth of May, some of his teammates teased him about taking too many pitches in the batting cage, and suggested he make room for the regulars. Hunter, who loves to hit, appealed to Kennedy, who told him to "get out of there." Kennedy laughed and said, "Pitchers can't hit."

Later, Hunter laughed and said, "That made me so mad I went out there and really bore down." He not only got three hits and knocked in three runs, but pitched the perfect game, which was a good way to attract attention to the A's in their new hometown.

By the time he got to the clubhouse, Charlie Finley was calling to tell him he'd earned a $5,000 bonus. Catcher Jim

Russ Reed, Oakland *Tribune*

Jim Hunter and young son, Todd.

A good-hitting pitcher, Catfish Hunter takes a big cut in batting practice.

Pagliaroni was given a grand. Chuck Dobson laughed and said, "There go our raises for next year."

Hunter presented Pagliaroni with an engraved gold watch worth another $1,000, and spread the credit around among his mates. He went home happily and the telephone started to ring.

Ken Smith of the Hall of Fame called at 8 the next morning to say they wanted his cap and winning ball. Catfish said they could have the uniform cap, but he wanted to keep the ball. He still has it, framed as a trophy.

He hurried out and bought all the newspapers he could find. "Ordinarily I don't read them," he admitted. "I learned long ago that a guy knows danged well how he has pitched, good or bad, and it messes you up to read the opinions of others. But I wanted to know what everyone had to say about this one.

"It was a thrill. It got my head to spinning," Hunter admitted later. It threw him off stride.

Before his next start, he was asked if he might try to tie Johnny Vander Meer's record.

"Who's Johnny Vander Meer?" the Catfish asked.

Vander Meer, he was told, was the only pitcher ever to throw consecutive no-hitters.

Every pitcher who pitches a no-hitter is asked about it and of course it's a meaningless question because theoretically every pitcher is trying to pitch a no-hitter every game. He doesn't want to give up the first hit. If he does, he doesn't want to give up the second. He doesn't want to give up a run. If he does, he doesn't want to give up a second. And so forth.

"If I can get it, I'll take it, but all I want is a win. A perfect game or a no-hitter is a dream come true, but twenty wins is the mark of the top pitcher," commented Catfish. "Whether it's a no-hitter or a ten-hitter, I'm happy if I win and I won't be content until I become a consistent twenty-game winner."

He did not come close to a no-hitter, but he did get a win in his next start. His no-hitter was spoiled by the first batter on Hunter's second pitch when Rod Carew hoisted it over the fence. Two-run homers by Tony Oliva and Rich Rollins followed. Before the first inning was finished Minnesota had Hunter hooked, 5–0.

But he hung in there and the A's rallied. They got two runs back in the second inning, another in the third, and six in the fourth to take the lead, 9–5. Hunter was hammered out in a three-run sixth that cut the score to 9–8, but he was bailed out by the bullpen and got credit for a 13–8 victory.

"It looks the same in the won-and-lost column as the other one," he observed.

However, he had been bent out of balance by his big game. He started trying to overpower the opposition to match that miracle and he lost his rhythm. He gave up home runs in almost all his starts and was hit hard at times. He started to fool around with his form and suffered two losing streaks.

He completed only 11 of 34 starts, but worked 234 innings, and concluded the campaign at 13–13 with a 3.35 ERA.

The next season he completed only 10 of 35 starts, worked 247 innings, and wound up with a 12–5 record and another 3.35 ERA.

It was as though he had improved to a plateau and could get no farther. But it was just a matter of time before he would begin to improve again.

"I had learned a lot, but I had to put it all together," he says. "I had reached my mid-twenties and I was maturing.

"The kind of pitcher I am, I have to concentrate on every pitch. If I don't put it right where I want it, they can hit it.

"My manager and pitching coach helped me settle into my motion. I'd pitch one way eight times, then another way the ninth time, and that's the one they'd hit.

"I'd lose concentration and start to think about my record or something, maybe how I had this game in the bag and that gave me so many wins, and I'd make a careless pitch and they'd hit it and I'd wind up with a loss instead.

"I got to where I shut everything else out of my mind but the next pitch and I became consistent.

"A little thing like learning to bend my knees smoothed out my form. Bending my right knee gave me a better push-off and bending my left knee gave me a better follow through. The good pitchers do it.

"I was becoming a good pitcher. I was better than my record. I'm a team pitcher. I need help. As my team got better and helped me more, my record got better."

The A's were becoming a good team by then. In 1968, for the first time, Finley's team won more than it lost, soaring to 82–80 and sixth place, though he fired the manager anyway. Bando, Jackson, and Monday gave the team a lift at the plate and in the field and flashed great talent. Blue Moon Odom blazed to 16 wins, while Hunter and Nash won 13 each and Chuck Dobson a dozen.

Divisional play was inaugurated in 1969 and the A's made a run at the pennant before settling for second place with an 88–74 record, 9 games behind Minnesota. Finley still was dissatisfied and ended Hank Bauer's second stint as his manager late in the year, replacing him with John McNamara.

But Jackson hit 47 homers and drove in 118 runs, Bando blasted 31 homers and drove home 113 runs, and Green and Campaneris sparkled afield. Odom and Dobson won 15 games each and Hunter 12. It was just a matter of time until this sort of talent told.

"We were all on the verge of big things by then," Hunter recalls.

8

Entering the 1970s, the Oakland A's and Catfish Hunter were reaching their peak.

In 1970, the A's finished second in their division for the second straight season and Hunter won more games than he lost for the first season. It was his sixth season and he won 18 games and lost 14. It was the most victories by an A's pitcher since the franchise shifted from Philadelphia to Kansas City fifteen years earlier. Catfish, of course, contends he would have won 20 had he not taken out a loan prior to the start of the season, then been badgered by owner Charles O. Finley for repayment through a winless month of August.

Reggie Jackson feuded with Finley throughout the season and neither he nor Sal Bando performed with the promise they had shown the previous season. Blue Moon Odom sagged with a sore arm. Chuck Dobson started swiftly, then he too sagged with a sore arm. There were some bright spots. First baseman Don Mincher hit 27 home runs. Shortstop Bert Campaneris stole 42 bases to lead the league for the fifth time in six seasons. Center fielder Rick Monday batted .290. Starter-reliever Diego Segui led the league in earned-run average at 2.56. Reliever Mudcat Grant won 6 games and saved 24, but his reward was to be traded before season's end. Vida Blue came up near season's end and threw a no-hitter.

And then there was Hunter, who finished only 9 of 40 starts and had a mediocre 3.81 ERA, but worked 262 innings and struggled through a series of close games with little support. He was superb at times. He was backed by

CATFISH   99

two runs or less five times and was involved in 11 one-run decisions, winning six. He won twice by 2–1, but lost twice by 2–1, another time by 2–0, another time by 3–2. "The stats don't show my progress in 1970," he said. "August ruined the numbers. Most of the year I was putting it together at last."

So was the team. After one season John McNamara was removed by Finley in favor of Dick Williams. Williams, who had won with the Red Sox, started to show the A's how to win. The team's record improved from 88–74 in 1969 and 89–73 in 1970 to 101–60 in 1971 and they swept to the divisional laurels by 16 games. Interest in Oakland increased, but not in proportion to a pennant-winning performance. From the 800,000 range on arrival in town, it had declined to the 700,000 range. Now it rose into the 900,000 area, but the team deserved more.

Jackson hit 32 homers and drove in 82 runs. He had 19 game-winning hits. Bando belted 24 homers and drove home 94 runs. Spare Tommy Davis hit .324. Green anchored an excellent inner defense. Campaneris stole 34 bases. Mincher had been traded for Mike Epstein and Darold Knowles. Epstein had 11 game-winning hits. Knowles saved 7 games. Rollie Fingers, taken off the starting staff in May and converted to relief, saved 17. Dobson won 15, but he and Odom suffered sore arms that made them ineffective at the finish. Blue and Hunter pitched the team to the top.

Blue was brilliant. For half a season he was as brilliant as a hurler has been in modern times. After losing his first start, Vida won 10 in a row. By mid-July he had won 18 and all were complete games. Seven were shutouts. He had a one-hitter, a two-hitter, and two three-hitters. He was spectacular, attractive, and new. He was in headlines, his handsome face on national magazine covers. Everyone wondered if he would win 30.

The pressure of his prominence altered his natural good nature and he began to feel scorched by the spotlight. He lost two 1–0 games in succession and started to press. Suffering from lack of support, he suddenly found it hard to win. He struggled through the stretch, but still finished with a 24–8 record and a 1.82 ERA, which won him both the Cy Young Award and the Most Valuable Player Trophy in the American League.

At the peak of his prominence, Blue was big at the box office and Finley ordered him saved for the best dates at home, even if it meant moving others out of the rotation in their turn. This hurt Hunter, who was having his best season, too, but was overshadowed.

Late in August, Hunter had 15 victories and was passed up in turn so Blue could pitch the much-publicized opener of a series with Boston. Rained out in Washington, it was Hunter's turn on Friday night in Oakland, but Blue was slated to start instead.

Asked about it, manager Williams said, "We sent Vida home early so he could pitch tonight, we advertised he'd pitch tonight, the fans expect him to pitch tonight, so he'll pitch tonight. Hunter understands."

Blue said, "I hope he understands. I'm sure some of my teammates are happy for me and some are jealous of me. It's human nature. They've worked hard for this for a long time, I come along and in one quick move I scrape off all the gravy. It's not fair, but I'm just doing what I'm told to do."

Hunter stood by his locker, looking at the crowd around Blue. He said, "I understand. I don't like it, but I understand. I'm having my best season, too. I've never won twenty and I have a chance to win twenty this year. I know I'm helping this club win the pennant. I like to pitch in turn and I think in the long run it's best for all concerned. So sometimes I cuss Vida under my breath. But that's nonsense. He doesn't have any say over it any more than I do. He's a working man like me and he does what they tell him to do.

"His situation this year is very sensational and very special and they have to accommodate it. I can see that. I can see how much more crowded the stands are when he pitches than when I pitch. And I can read the stats, too, and I know he's earned some of this. It's not easy to take, though. I can't say it is."

Blue pitched and lost that night, 1–0. Hunter pitched and won the next afternoon, 4–1. Both gave up one run, but Blue got no runs and Hunter got four. In their next starts, Blue lost 1–0 again and Hunter lost 4–2. Blue lost a couple of more times before the season ended, but Hunter did not lose again.

The Catfish won in Washington, 9–0. He won in Minnesota, 5–4. He blanked the Angels, 1–0. He was the A's ace through the stretch. He won his twentieth game in Kansas City in 11 innings, 2–1, to clinch a tie for the pennant, and two days later the team clinched the pennant. Before the season ended, Hunter won again over K.C., 2–1.

He didn't win his first game until his fourth start, but wound up with a 21–11 record and a 2.96 ERA. He had finished 16 of 37 starts and fired 5 shutouts. His 181 strikeouts could not be compared to Blue's 301, but as the season wore on, Catfish was the consistent star of the staff, not Vida. But the A's didn't realize that then.

As the play-offs approached, everyone around the A's was counting on Blue to pitch the team to the top. How many could he win? How many starts would he get? was the answer. The pressure pounded at him. "I don't want to think about it," he admitted. Then he had to do it.

In the opener in Baltimore, Blue blanked the Orioles for three innings and was given a 3–0 lead and the A's seemed on their way. Back-to-back doubles brought Baltimore a run in the fourth. Heading into the home half of the seventh, Blue was sailing along on a three-hitter with a 3–1 lead. Then a walk, two ground balls that went for singles, and two balls bounced down the left-field line that went for doubles and he was behind, 5–3, and beaten.

The A's seemed to sag. Hunter, too. They had banked a lot on Blue and he had been beaten. They had banked too much on Blue and they were beaten now. Hunter didn't have it in the second game and the A's were beaten, 5–1.

Two home runs by Boog Powell and one each by Brooks Robinson and Elrod Hendricks caved in the Catfish, though he went the route.

Back in Oakland, the Orioles wrapped it up, 5–3, despite two home runs by Reggie Jackson. As the A's walked slowly from the dugout to their dressing room in despair, Jackson remained slumped on the dugout steps for five minutes, his head hidden in his arms, before he could bring himself to go.

In that tomb of a dressing room, a disappointed Catfish Hunter said, "We used up everything we had getting here. We just didn't save enough. Just getting here seemed like something to us. Now we know it's nothing unless you go on to the World Series. Now we've been here once. We know what it is. We'll be back. We'll be ready next time. We know what we have to do now."

The A's did bounce back. They overcame one obstacle after another en route to a second straight divisional title. Veterans Orlando Cepeda and Denny McLain were brought in by Finley and flopped. Blue battled Finley for a better contract, lost, reported late, and flopped. Surgery sidelined Chuck Dobson. Dick Green was hurt most of the season and on orders from Charlie O, Williams used 11 different second basemen, including outfielders and catchers, pinch-hitting for each as he came up. However, the A's had started to swagger. Following a mustache-day promotion, they had hair all over their faces and performed like pirates. They fought among themselves and then pulled together to fight and defeat foes. They fought off the opposition in the final month to win going away.

Epstein hit 26 homers and Jackson 25. No one drove in 100 runs, but five of the A's drove in 70 or more. Catchers Dave Duncan and Gene Tenace drove in more than 90 between them. Joe Rudi arrived with a .305. He scored 94 runs. Campaneris recaptured the stolen-base crown with 52 and scored 85 runs.

The A's pitchers made the most of the runs provided them. The bullpen backed up the starters beautifully. Fin-

Ron Riesterer, Oakland *Tribune*

Reggie Jackson sits slumped in dugout, reluctant to depart after disappointing final defeat at the hands of the Orioles in the 1971 American League play-offs.

After being hit by pitched ball, Campy Campaneris starts to throw bat at Detroit hurler in 1972 play-off rhubarb.

gers won 11 games and saved 21. Knowles won 5 and saved 11. Hunter led the starters. He won 21 and lost only 7. He was the first of the A's to record back to back 20-victory seasons since Lefty Grove 39 years earlier. Acquired along with Billy North in a trade for Rick Monday, left-hander Ken Holtzman won 19 and lost only 11. Blue Moon Odom won 15 and lost only 6.

Hunter established himself as the star starter. Offered $45,000 in salary for the season, he asked an additional $5,000 for his .350 batting average of the year before and was given it. Again he hit hard all year, but it was his pitching that paid off.

Again he started slowly. He did not win his first game until the end of the season's first month, when he five-hit Milwaukee, 2–1. His record was only 2–2 after six weeks. But he was steady after that. His second win was 4–1, a five-hitter versus visiting New York. His first shutout was 2–0 at Baltimore. He allowed only two hits and didn't walk a man. This came early in June and was the 100th victory of his eight-season pro career. His parents and others of his family watched proudly from the stands.

Midway in June, he lost a heartbreaker to Baltimore in 10 innings, 2–1, but in his next start, he won over Detroit in 11 innings, 3–2. "You win some tough ones and you lose some. If you pitch well, you'll win your share," he said with a shrug. He had become a pro, performing consistently in good times and bad. Next out, he stifled the Angels, 6–1, on three hits, getting two hits himself. In Anaheim, he blanked the Angels, 5–0, on two hits.

On the eighth of July he won his tenth, a five-hit, 7–0 shutout of Milwaukee. He stretched his streak of shutout innings to 24 before it was broken in New York, but he still beat the Yankees, 9–3. He gave up two hits and three runs in the first inning, but bore down and surrendered only one hit and no runs the rest of the way. In 32 of his last 33 innings he had shut out the opposition.

At midseason, manager Williams commented, "He has become our top pitcher, our stopper, the best in baseball. He has good stuff, but more important he knows how to use it. He is very smart and very tough. He may not impress you in a given game the way a Vida Blue or a Jim Palmer will at their best, but if you see him in a season's worth of games, you have to be impressed. He is a real pro."

Commented the Catfish, "I always thought I could do it. The difference is now I know I can do it. Every time out. If I do have a bad outing, I'm confident I'll come back with a good one next time out. I have complete confidence now. Our entire team has confidence. We help each other. We know we can win. We expect to win, which most teams don't."

In Milwaukee he blanked the Brewers, 4–0. He gave up five hits and one walk. One walk per game was about par for his pitching now. He wasn't giving anything away. In Boston he was in constant trouble, but hung on to win, 5–3, on a nine-hitter. His hot stretch was snapped at 42 shutout innings out of 43, but still he won.

Around the start of August, Hunter, Holtzman, and Blue pitched three straight shutout victories for the A's. Hunter's was a five-hitter versus the Royals. He allowed just one walk. Naturally.

After his fifteenth victory he announced he wanted to be the highest-paid pitcher on the A's. He said it simply, without bragging. He had become the ace of the staff and knew it. He merited more than Blue. Or the newcomer Holtzman. "I deserve it," he said. "I have become the top pitcher on our staff. If I don't get the top salary, I'll ask to get traded."

"He'll be taken care of," Finley harumphed. "Just let him keep on winning." Hunter kept on winning and won a raise to $85,000 for the following year from Finley. That was more than the others were earning. Not much more, but more.

When the A's slumped slightly and fell from the top position late in August, it was Hunter who won for them at Detroit, 5–1, to put them back into a tie for first place with the White Sox.

He came back against Cleveland to shut out the Indians,

An ecstatic Charlie Finley celebrates with the players' wives
after World Series success.

Russ Reed, Oakland *Tribune*

Charlie Finley greets the fans in Oakland as Sal Bando, left, and Jim Hunter, center, hold the title trophy.

1–0, on four hits. By mid-September when he won his twentieth, a two-hit, one-walk, 4–1 triumph over the Royals, the
team had pulled away again in the pennant race.

His twenty-first victory came at month's end, a 2–1 trim-
ming of visiting Minnesota. At season's end, he had lost
only seven. One was by 1–0. Another by 2–1. Another by
3–2. In three of his losses, his side was shut out. He completed 16 of 37 starts again, but that was because the A's
had a brilliant bullpen. He had his best-ever earned-run-
average, 2.04. He had six shutouts. He struck out 191 and
walked only 70 in 295 innings.

The A's won-and-lost had fallen off to 93–62, but they
were ready for the play-offs this season. "We've saved something," Catfish said. "We don't waste wins. We only win
what we have to win. We don't get a lot of hits or runs, but
we don't waste what we get and we win. That is the way you
win in postseason play. We're ready to win the play-offs this
time. We'll win the World Series, too. We're ready."

This time it was the Cat, not Vida, who was the A's key
man. And he was ready for that sort of responsibility.

The A's were ready. Knowles broke his left thumb late in
the season and was sidelined the entire postseason period.
Campaneris was struck by a pitch, threw his bat at pitcher
Lerrin LaGrow in the second game, and was suspended the
last three games of the five-game play-offs with Detroit.
Reggie Jackson pulled a muscle sliding home in the final
game and was sidelined the rest of the game and the World
Series with Cincinnati. Nine of the 12 postseason contests
were decided by one run and the A's won six of them. They
won the big ones.

Hunter hurled the opener of the play-offs and the A's
beat Baltimore. He didn't get the decision, but deserved it,
leaving in the eighth inning after surrendering only four
hits, two walks, and one run. Blue bailed him out of a jam
and Fingers finished it off. Mickey Lolich was beaten in the
eleventh, 3–2.

Odom blanked Detroit, 5–0, in the second game. But the
Tigers, managed by Billy Martin, rallied to tie the series.

They trimmed Holtzman and the A's, 3–0, in the third game, then went 11 innings to win 4–3, in the fourth. Again Hunter did not get a decision, again leaving in the eighth after allowing only six hits, three walks, and one run.

Blue bailed out Odom as the A's nosed out the Tigers, 2–1, in the decisive contest in Detroit. Afterward, Blue baited Odom for not finishing what he had started and the two tangled in what should have been a happy dressing room. But that was the way of the A's. And they were on their way to the World Series.

The first two games were in Cincinnati. It was Holtzman's turn to start and he started the opener. He got help from Fingers and Blue and with two home runs by Tenace trimmed the Reds, 3–2.

Rudi's home run in the third turned out to be the winner as Hunter stifled the Reds in the second game, 2–1. Cat got help from Fingers, too. Cat had shut out the Reds on four hits entering the last of the ninth. He was wearing out. Tony Perez singled to left. Denis Menke lined to left, but Rudi made a leaping, backhanded catch against the fence. Cesar Geronimo bounced out to first, but Hal McRae bounced a single to left, scoring a run. Fingers came on and retired Julian Javier on a foul fly off first to finish it off.

It turned out that Hunter's 8 2/3 innings were the closest an A's pitcher would come to a complete game in three straight World Series.

Hunter held the winning ball in the clubhouse later, symbolic of his first World Series victory, smiled, and said, "We help each other. I'm happy to have had help when I needed it. I'll take the victories any way I can get them. I think I could have gotten the last out, but Rollie got it so I can't complain. I wanted the complete game, but with our bullpen you have to take a tired starter out sometimes. I wanted the complete game, but not as much as I wanted the victory." All around him the A's were hollering happily.

Finley, his family, and his friends had hollered happily throughout the game, waving A's pennants. On the flight home for the next three games, he strutted up and down the aisles of the airplane, congratulating his team as though it had already won the World Series. When he congratulated Dave Duncan and started to embrace him happily, Duncan drew back and said, in selected words, he wanted no part of the owner. Shocked, Charlie drew back. A lot of the A's laughed. That was their way. But Duncan's days with the A's were numbered then.

Again, only about 900,000 fans had turned out for the A's all season. Only around 30,000 fans had turned out for each of the two play-off games in Oakland. However, just over 50,000 had attended each World Series game in Cincinnati, and, swept up in the fever of the fall classic, just under 50,000 would attend each classic contest in Oakland. It didn't matter to the A's. They played for themselves, not their fans and not their owner. They called the cold Coliseum "the Mausoleum." The Catfish laughed: "It's not much, but it's ours."

Jack Billingham blanked the A's as the Reds got a run off Odom and won one, 1–0, in Tuesday night's game. But the next night, Tenace hit another homer and the A's, behind Holtzman, Blue, and Fingers, triumphed, 3–2, to take a three-games-to-one lead in the series and move within one of wrapping it up.

Pete Rose opened the fifth game with a home run off the first pitch from the Catfish, but Tenace hit a three-run home run, his fourth homer of the series, to put the A's ahead in the second inning. Menke hit a homer in the fourth. Tolan singled in a run in the fifth. Williams lifted Hunter, although he led, 4–3. Fingers relieved and lost it in the late innings, 5–4.

"The way Hunter hangs in there, it was a mistake," Jackson said, and a lot of the A's agreed.

So they went back to Cincinnati and the A's blasted Blue and won, 8–1, to tie the Series and send it into a seventh, decisive game. It was Odom's start, but Hunter and Holtzman went to the bullpen because there was no tomorrow. And, after the A's took an early lead, Hunter had to help Odom out of a jam in the fifth.

He got McRae and Perez on fly balls, though the first fetched in a run to tie the count. Tenace and Bando doubled in runs in the sixth. Hunter blanked the Reds in the sixth and seventh. When he gave up a single to Rose to start the eighth, Williams went to Holtzman. When Holtzman gave up a double to Morgan, Williams went to Fingers.

Perez flied for one run, but Rollie retired them in order after that. As the Reds and their disappointed fans drifted off, the A's came together in jubilation and hurried to their dressing room to celebrate with champagne the franchise's first world title since 1930, when the team was in Philadelphia and Connie Mack was the boss.

Now Charlie O. Finley kept stepping between the players and the spotlight as the celebration hit its height. Hunter and Bando carried the heavy little trophy between them as the party transferred to the plane for the trip back to Oakland. Here, about 12,000 fans awaited them at the airport. Finley mounted the podium and stood with outstretched hands, receiving the cheers of the crowd. Someone said, "Good God, he's going to proclaim himself king."

He did not, but he treated his winners royally. He added $1,500 diamond-studded championship rings to the winners' World Series shares of more than $20,000 each. "The money is nice, but winning means more than money. Most players play their entire careers without playing in a World Series, much less winning one. Winning this one has to be the thrill of a lifetime for me. Nothing could top it," Catfish Hunter said.

"How about winning another one, next year?"

"Wouldn't that be something?" He smiled. "Maybe we will, I think. But it couldn't top this."

It couldn't.

9

The true test of a champion is that he wins not just once, but more than once. Many win once, few can continue to win. Once the thirst has been quenched, the hunger abated, it takes tremendous desire and talent to stay at the top, it takes strength of character and personal pride to win again and again.

The old Yankees had it. The Green Bay Packers. The Montreal Canadiens. The Boston Celtics. Each sport has had one or two and they stand out above all others, having made a mark above and beyond the usual. In the 1970s the Oakland A's made one of those lasting marks which will stand.

Of all of the A's, Jim "Catfish" Hunter stood out as the one who contributed most consistently through their championship seasons.

In 1973, the A's won their third straight divisional title with a 94–68 mark, six games to the good over Kansas City.

Leading the way were 20 twenty-game winners—Hunter at 21–5, Holtzman at 21–3, and Blue, bouncing back, at 20–9. Fingers won 7 and saved 22.

In support, Jackson hit 32 home runs and drove in 117 runs, Bando hit 29 homers and drove in 98 runs and Tenace hit 24 homers and drove in 84 runs. Billy North stole 53 bases and Campaneris 34. Green glued a good defense. Rudi suffered from injuries, but others bore the burden.

Again, Hunter had a slow start. He was bombed in an 8–3 opening-game defeat and did not win a game until his sixth start at the end of the first month, when he shut out Baltimore until the ninth and hung on to top them, 4–3, on four hits, with help from Fingers.

113

However, in May and June he had a streak in which he allowed only two runs in five victories, blanking the Angels 4–0 and the Royals, 5–0, whipping the Red Sox, 3–1, and the Brewers 11–1, and blanking the Tigers, 5–0. The last was a three-hitter with only one walk.

"He is pitching at his peak," marveled Williams.

"I am the best I have been," admitted the Cat.

Late in June Kansas City came to Oakland, threatening the A's hold on the divisional lead. Hunter turned them back, 3–2. He gave up two runs in the third, toughened, and blanked them the rest of the way while the A's rallied to win.

By the All-Star Game break late in July, Hunter was the hottest pitcher in the majors with a 15–3 record. As usual he was surrendering home runs, but they weren't hurting him. He'd given up nine homers in his last four starts, but was riding the wave of a 10-game winning streak.

He was honored by being selected to start the star-filled classic for the American League in Kansas City and retired the first four batters to face him—Pete Rose, Joe Morgan, Cesar Cedeno, and Hank Aaron—before Billy Williams hit a ball right back at him. Trying to bare-hand the ball, the Catfish suffered a fracture of his right thumb.

The A's were shocked, but Hunter took it stoically. "Heck, I need the rest and it might help me," he said with a shrug. "I'll be strong for August and September and that's when we're going to need it the most."

Only then did he disclose that he had suffered bone-chip fractures of his left thumb and ring finger when hit by a baseball in pregame warm-ups in Baltimore in May.

"I didn't want to say anything because I didn't want to be sidelined," he said. "This now will be the first scheduled starts I've missed since my appendectomy in 1966 and those were the only ones in my major league career.

"It happens." He shrugged. "I'm not bitter about it. People say it's a shame it had to happen in an All-Star Game. I don't look at it that way. The All-Star Game may not mean much to the players, but it does to the fans, and they're the ones who pay our salaries.

Russ Reed, Oakland *Tribune*

Second baseman Mike Andrew sorrowfully scuffs ground after making one of the errors in the 1973 World Series against the Mets that angered Charlie Finley and touched off a storm.

An angry Charlie O. Finley after American League president Joe Cronin delayed the fourth game of the 1973 play-offs against the Orioles one day because of rain.

"I know if I lived in Kansas City or any city where the All-Star Game was to be played and I was a fan instead of a player I'd go crazy to buy a ticket to see all the best players from both leagues on one field at one time.

"I'm proud to have been picked as one of the best and honored to have gotten to be the starting pitcher for my side and an accident isn't going to change my feelings about that," Catfish concluded.

They splinted his thumb and waited for him to heal. While he was out, the A's lost the lead, regained it, struggled to hold on to it. Hunter started to throw the ball within one week, but he hurt his thumb and had to quit for a while.

He was out twenty-five days before he returned in mid-August, working five innings of a 6–4 win over Milwaukee, leaving with a 4–2 lead. On the twenty-fourth, one month to the day from his injury, he won his sixteenth decision of the season, working seven innings of a 5–1 victory. Four nights later he beat Boston for his seventeenth, working seven innings of a 6–1 victory. In the latter, he allowed only one hit.

It was with a sigh of relief that Williams and the A's welcomed their ace's return to the rotation and the A's started to pull away again.

His twentieth came tough. Before the game, pitching coach Wes Stock wondered if Hunter's thumb still hurt him. But Hunter had heard all he wanted to hear about that thumb and hollered that at the coach.

In the game he gave up a homer in the first inning, then back-to-back homers in the fourth and the Angels started to ride him. Even his catcher, Ray Fosse, rode him. "You're not throwing hard," he told his pitcher at the mound.

When the next batter stepped up, Billy Parker, Hunter threw hard—high and inside—and the hitter went sprawling in the dirt to avoid being beaned.

"That was a purpose pitch," manager Williams said with a smile later. "That was the best pitch of the inning."

"I got a little ticked off," Hunter admitted later. "I got tough."

Ron Riesterer, Oakland *Tribune*

Reggie Jackson jumps on home plate after his home run put
the A's ahead of the Mets in the final game of the 1973 World
Series.

He blanked the Angels after that, beating them, 5–4.

Afterward someone observed he now had given up 35 home runs that season, the most he'd surrendered in a single season.

"I don't care how many homers I give up as long as I win," the Cat said with a growl.

After concluding his campaign with his twenty-first victory, Hunter was asked about his chances of winning the Cy Young Award.

"I'd like to win it, but it doesn't make that much difference to me," he said.

He had won 21 games for the third straight season. Over those three seasons he had won 63 games and lost only 23. He had led the league in winning percentage for the second straight season.

"I think sometimes it's given for several seasons, but I think it should be based on the one season only," he observed. "They give an award every season, after all."

This season, his 21–5 mark and 3.34 ERA could be compared to Jim Palmer's 22–9 and 2.40 ERA and Nolan Ryan's 21–16 and 2.87. Ryan also set a major league mark with 383 strikeouts.

Who was the best pitcher? "I don't think I'm the best pitcher. I don't know who is. I think I'm one of the best," Catfish commented. "I'm consistent. So is Palmer. Ryan throws the hardest. He'd win more with a better club, but you can't count that. I'd have won more if I hadn't been hurt, but I was.

"I think Burt Blyleven has the best stuff, but he makes too many mistakes so he doesn't win enough and loses too much. What matters the most is on the bottom line, wins or losses. You work with what you've got to work with.

"I want to win the Cy Young Award, but I'd rather win the play-offs," the Catfish concluded.

Palmer won the Cy Young Award, but his Baltimore team was beaten by Hunter's A's in the play-offs.

The first two games were played in Baltimore. It was Blue's turn so he started, but he was bombed out in the first frame and the Orioles, who had closed the campaign with ten consecutive victories, went on to win behind Palmer, 6–0. Clearly the A's reign was threatened. They turned to the Catfish. He scattered seven hits and with help from Fingers snapped the Oriole streak, 6–3.

The best-of-five series shifted to Oakland for the final games. The A's finally had topped 1,000,000 attendance for a season, but not by much. More than 30,000 turned out for the third game. Less than 30,000 for the fourth game. Less than 25,000 for the final game, the lowest in the history of play-offs.

"I don't count the crowd, only the victories," Hunter said. Their victory in the third game took eleven innings. Holtzman nipped Mike Cuellar, 2–1. Holtzman gave three hits, Cuellar four. A homer by little Campaneris settled it.

Joe Cronin, American League president, postponed the game one day due to rain. Finley attacked him verbally.

Victory eluded the A's in the fourth game. The Orioles sent Palmer out to tie up the series, but he was knocked out in the second inning. Baltimore rallied to rout Blue and beat Fingers, 5–4. Afterward Fingers berated Blue and was challenged by Odom before they were parted.

That put it to a fifth and final game and the A's sent Hunter out to win the series. He did, shutting out the Orioles, 3–0. He went the distance, scattering five hits and two walks.

He didn't permit the visitors to mount a threat all night.

Afterward a writer observed, "Curious talent, this Catfish. He's not physically impressive. He doesn't throw especially hard. He doesn't sound all that smart. In fact, the A's would probably drop him if he didn't win twenty games every year. And the big games at the end of every year."

In the winners' dressing room, manager Williams said, "He has to be the best in baseball. He does the most when it counts the most. And he does it almost every time out." Captain Bando added, "Hunter has more guts than any guy in the game. He's just great."

Hunter said, simply, "It's good to win. Now the World Series."

Finley was in a fury as the fall classic commenced. Ac-

Ron Riesterer, Oakland *Tribune*

The A's mob Darrold Knowles after he got the final out of the fall classic.

cording to the rules, he needed the permission of his foe to add any players to his roster prior to the Series. Twice he asked the Mets for permission to add Manny Trillo, an obscure infielder, and twice he was refused. After the second refusal, he had it announced sarcastically during the opening game in Oakland. The Mets were booed by the A's fans and Finley was reprimanded by Bowie Kuhn.

The A's won that first game, 2–1, as Holtzman, with help from the bullpen, beat Jon Matlack. But they lost the second game, 11–7, as both starters, Blue and Jerry Koosman, were routed. It went twelve innings and two errors by Mike Andrews helped the Mets to their four runs in the final frame. Williams was using the Finley plan of pinch-hitting for his second baseman. Andrews was the third of the day. He was playing for the first time since August.

After the game, Finley met with Andrews and Dr. Walker in a closed session that produced a statement from the player that he was withdrawing from the Series with a shoulder injury, presumably permitting Trillo to replace him. The A's were outraged. Hunter said, "I can't believe that Mike would quit during a World Series. This had to be Finley's doing, and it's the worst thing Finley could do. Mike said he might quit at the end of the season, anyway, but this was no way to go. You feel especially sorry for him because he was a good guy, but it could happen to any of us, and we know it." They gathered angrily to discuss the incident during their plane flight to New York. After their arrival, their anger increased when they read reports from Andrews that he had been pressured into issuing an untrue statement and into leaving the team. Then Williams confided to them this was "the final straw" and he was resigning after the Series. The A's threatened a strike, but were pacified when Kuhn reprimanded Finley and ordered Andrews reinstated. Andrews did rejoin the team, but considerable damage had been done.

"We were pros so we were going to play. We're proud, so we were going to play to win. But the pleasure had been taken from it by Finley. Whatever else he had done, this

James Roark, Los Angeles *Herald-Examiner*

The Catfish is greeted by manager Alvin Dark and teammates after another pitching triumph in 1974 Series.

Between bidding sessions, home state hero Hunter signs autographs for local youngsters. Note, lower part of the picture, someone has brought program for his signature from 1937 All-Star Game, almost ten years before Jim was born.

was the worst. He had spoiled something for us that would never be the same again," admitted Hunter.

He was unsettled as he took the mound for the third game. His second pitch was smacked into the seats by Wayne Garrett. Two singles and a wild pitch produced a second run. Hunter fussed on the mound, getting a grip on himself. He put everything but his pitches out of his mind. He blanked the Mets on three hits from then through the sixth inning, when he was lifted for a pinch hitter. The bullpen took over and Paul Lindblad got the victory as the A's rallied to win in eleven, 3–2. It was another of his superb pitching performances in postseason play which went unrewarded in the victory column and does not show in the statistics. "It doesn't matter that I didn't win," he said with a shrug later. "The team won, which is what matters. This team wins on the field no matter what happens off the field. Hard times seem to bring out the best in us. We're a hard group of guys."

In the clubhouse behind him, Odom hollered, "Dissention does it again."

Odom was savaged by the surprising Mets in the fourth game and the New Yorkers won, 6–1, behind Matlack, to even the series at two victories each. Williams went back to Blue for the fifth game and he worked well, but he lost his seventh straight play-off or World Series start, 2–0, to Koosman and reliever Tug McGraw. Met fans celebrated as if they had captured the classic. Down three games to two, the A's flew home knowing they had to win two straight in Oakland to hang onto their title. Sellout crowds of near 50,000 awaited them for both games. Jackson, who had been having a bad series, said, "I thought I was a stud who wouldn't feel pressure, but I feel it now." Asked about Hunter, who would pitch, Jackson said, "He doesn't feel pressure." Against Tom Seaver? "Against anyone," Jackson said. "Seaver is super, but he isn't Hunter."

It was the game the A's had to win and Hunter won it for them. Jackson doubled in runs in the first and third innings and the Catfish shut out the Mets on three hits and one walk for seven innings. With one out in the eighth, Boswell singled for the fourth hit off Hunter and Williams, with that quick hook, lifted him and inserted Knowles. After Felix Millan singled in a run, Williams lifted Knowles and inserted Fingers. It was finished off at 3–1 and the classic went to a final contest.

After his fifth fine World Series showing, Hunter had his third victory. Sitting, sweaty but satisfied, in the dressing room afterward, the Cat said, shrugging, "We don't believe in complete games on this team, but we do believe in victories."

That left it to Holtzman and Matlack for the decisive game. Two-run homers by Campaneris and Jackson finished off the Mets in the fourth. With the help of two spectacular catches by Jackson, Holtzman held the Mets until the sixth when Fingers bailed him out. Knowles, naturally, completed it. He appeared in each game.

When Knowles got Garrett on a pop to end it at 5–2, the A's streamed into their dressing room for a subdued celebration. Finley embraced Williams in front of the TV cameras and wished him well. Jackson jumped in. Reggie revealed he'd played under the pressure of an anonymous death threat received in the mails.

Told he had won the MVP award for the classic, Jackson commented, "Campaneris deserved it." Campaneris said, "I deserved it." Knowles said, "Maybe I did." Hunter said, "Let's go home." He was hunting by the time his winners' share of almost $25,000 was sent him.

When he went into contract negotiations before the 1973 season and settled for $75,000, he remembered Blue's holdout hassle and said, "I'll face Finley by myself. When you go in with someone else, the owner figures the lawyer gets some of the money. I'll never get a lawyer to negotiate a contract. I might get more money, but in the long run I wouldn't because I'd have to pay the lawyer." Many A's took Finley to arbitration and most were awarded what they wanted.

When he went into contract negotiations before the 1974

James Roark, Los Angeles *Herald-Examiner*

The Catfish, now mustachioed, in action.

season and settled for $100,000, Hunter again faced Finley alone. Again, many A's took Finley to arbitration, but this time most had to settle for what Finley had offered. Nevertheless, Jackson spoke for most of A's when he said, "The Cat is the most underpaid player on this team. A lot of us are making more. He should be making the most."

Hunter shrugged and said, "As long as I am being treated fairly, I can't complain." However, as the season progressed and payments into his pension plan were not made according to his contract, he began to brood and feel he was being treated unfairly. He started to think maybe he needed a lawyer after all, and eventually consulted an attorney in Ahoskie who had done business with him before.

Meanwhile, he performed professionally.

As usual, he started slowly. In mid-June his record read only 8–8. But he won 17 of his next 21 decisions in a consistent streak of sustained excellence that carried the club to its fourth consecutive divisional title. He started 41 games, completed 23, and worked a career-high 318 innings. He walked only 46 batters and was the only pitcher in the league to give up less walks and hits than innings he worked. His earned-run average of 2.49 was tops on the tour.

Hunter hurled six shutouts. The first came early in May when he blanked Cleveland, 5–0, on five hits and two walks. Late in June he blanked Kansas City, 4–0, on five hits and no walks. Early in July he blanked Baltimore, 6–0, on seven hits and two walks, and Cleveland, 7–0, on three hits and three walks in back-to-back shutouts, stifling Texas, 3–0, and Kansas City, 7–0, giving up four hits and not giving up a walk in each contest.

The Catfish had become the complete pitcher.

Other A's also were outstanding. Jackson hit 29 home runs and drove in 93 runs. Bando hit 22 home runs and drove in 103 runs. Rudi hit 22 home runs and drove in 99 runs. Tenace hit 26 home runs. North stole 54 bases, Campaneris 34, and Herb Washington, the pinch-running specialist controversially employed by Finley and new manager Alvin Dark, 29. Green was spectacular afield.

But Hunter had to have his best year for the A's to win another year. His 25–12 mark was by far the best on the staff. Holtzman won 19, but lost 17. Blue won 17, but lost 15. Only the ever-reliable Rollie Fingers also performed effectively, winning 9 games and saving 18 in a league-leading 76 appearances.

Of course, it was a typically tumultuous season for the Angry A's. Disappointed by the departure of Williams, the A's did not smile on his successor, Dark. Back for his second stint under Finley after a prolonged period out of the game, Alvin was out of touch. He had gotten religion, but the players ridiculed his quotes from the Bible. They laughed when Finley altered Alvin's lineups. They laughed at his mistakes until they hurt. The pitchers complained about his quick-hook tactics. The regulars rebelled at his handling of game situations. Bando blasted him in one publicized clubhouse incident. The players met and decided they could win despite him. "Finley manages this team, anyway," Jackson said with a sigh.

Jackson battled Blue Moon, and Fosse suffered an injury breaking it up. Finley flew in to rap Reggie in a clubhouse clash. Reggie brooded, then telephoned Charlie and told him off. Life went on. Charlie fired half the coaching staff. When he finally released Williams to replace Bobby Winkles as manager of the Angels, Charley brought in Bobby as coach of the A's. Finley flew in to give his team a pep talk when Kansas City closed in. The players laughed behind his back, then beat back Kansas City. They won 90 games, lost 72 and finished five in front of Texas.

Hunter won his twentieth game, 3–1, over Milwaukee, before August ran out. It was his fourth straight season with 20 or more victories. He won his twenty-fifth late in September, 2–1, over Minnesota, the first A's pitcher to win 25 games since Lefty Grove did it in Philadelphia in 1932. And it wrapped up a record fourth consecutive divisional title for the team. It clinched a title tie at the time and became the decisive game before the A's played again as Texas lost its next game.

Considering the race for Most Valuable Player honors, Reggie Jackson observed, "Jeff Burroughs will win because he has had the best season by a player other than pitchers, but I believe a player who has helped his side win the pennant is the true MVP. I will get votes, but I wouldn't vote for me. I'd vote for Bando or Rudi. The pitchers have their own award, but when you get right down to it, Fingers is as valuable as anyone in this league. Hunter, too. I think I would give Cat the Cy Young Award, the Most Valuable Player Award, the Academy Award, and the kitchen sink."

Burroughs won the MVP, but Hunter won the Young.

"I can't complain." Catfish shrugged. "I'd have liked to have won the MVP, but everyone is entitled to their opinion. I'm happy to have won the Cy Young, but awards don't mean much to me. I prefer another pennant and World Series win."

Which the Amazing A's won.

Hunter didn't have it in the opener at home with Baltimore. Three home runs helped the Orioles to six runs before they finished him in the fifth and went on to win, 6–3. The A's were shocked. As Jackson said later, "I was surprised Cat could get knocked out early like that. It stunned me. It stunned us. Well, he's entitled to a bad game, even in a big game like that. We've got to battle back."

They did. Holtzman evened the set with a five-hit, 5–0 win. Then in Baltimore, breaking his streak of postseason failures, Blue was brilliant, blanking the Orioles on two hits and beating Jim Palmer, 1–0.

The ball was handed to Hunter to wrap it up in the fourth game.

Commented Jackson, "I don't believe the Catfish can have another bad game. I think he's fabulous and I am counting on him to come through for us." He did. He shut out the Orioles on three hits and two walks for seven innings. Fingers finished out the last two innings, surrender-

James Roark, Los Angeles *Herald- Examiner*

He lays down and beats out a bunt against the Dodgers' Al Downing in the 1974 World Series.

James Roark, Los Angeles *Herald-Examiner*

ing one run in the ninth, but the A's won, 2–1, on one hit, a double by Jackson, and 11 walks off of Mike Cuellar and Ross Grimsley.

So the A's had their third straight American League pennant. "It means nothing if we don't win the World Series again, too," commented the Catfish.

First, of course, they had to set the stage. Andrews announced a lawsuit against Finley for depriving him of his profession by demeaning his standing in it. And a reporter discovered and wrote that Hunter was suing Finley for release from his contract, contending the owner had violated it. To top it off, Fingers and Blue Moon battled in the clubhouse and Reggie ripped into writer Murray Olderman on the field.

Clearly, the club was set to go.

The Catfish claimed, "None of this stuff bothers the A's. We've been through it before and won in spite of it. We're rowdy off the field, but professionals on it. We make the plays you have to make to win and we make them under pressure.

"The lawsuit won't bother me. I've got a job to do and I'll go out and do it. The court case comes later. The World Series is now. When I put on this uniform, I give one hundred percent. I don't care if it's in a cow pasture or a stadium full of people.

"There's some money to be made out there and I'm gonna go out and help us make it. Will Finley be rooting for me? You can bet on it. He wants the money as bad as I do. But if they didn't give you a dime for winning, I'd want to win. We all would. That's why we're champs."

Holtzman started the first game against the Dodgers in Los Angeles and Fingers came on in mid-game to help him out. Jackson's homer had helped the A's to a 3–2 lead, but when Garvey singled with two out in the ninth, Dark went to Hunter.

He'd been in the bullpen because he was not slated to start for two games and was ready to relieve if needed. He came in and struck out Joe Ferguson for the final out.

Catfish Hunter celebrates his World Series pitching triumph with slugger Reggie Jackson, left, and manager Dick Williams.

Later, Ferguson said, "He didn't show me anything." Jackson said, "The Cat never shows anyone anything, he just beats them." The Cat said, "I'm not trying to put on a show. I'm just trying to help us win."

Don Sutton and Mike Marshall beat Blue, 3–2, to tie the series, which then shifted to Oakland. Although regular-season attendance had dipped below 900,000, sellouts awaited them.

Here, Hunter held the Dodgers scoreless on four hits and two walks for seven innings in another powerful pressure performance. When Bill Buckner homered with one out in the eighth, Fingers was fetched. He surrendered a homer in the ninth, but held on to win, 3–2.

Afterward Hunter sat in his underwear in the winners' dressing room, sweat beading on his mustache, and he said, "It doesn't matter that I didn't finish, only that we won. I've said this before and I'll say it again. This is a team game and I'm only a part of our team. With a Fingers fresh in the bullpen, it would be foolish to take a chance on a tired start-er.

"It was a big game because it put us ahead. As long as we're ahead, we can't lose. No one likes to lose, but we like it less than most, which is maybe why we win more than most. I had a job to do and I did it. We've got a job to finish and we'll finish it."

They did, fast, despite talk by the Dodgers the A's were "lucky."

Holtzman hit a home run and with help from Fingers won the fourth game, 5–2.

It was Blue's turn to pitch the fifth game, which would be the final one if the A's could win it. An announcer asked Jackson about Blue and Reggie said, "Well, hell, I'd rather have Hunter, but I'm happy with Blue. I mean anyone would rather have Hunter in a game like this.

"It's like saying Seaver is going today, but I'd rather have Koufax. Well, Koufax could do it when it counts and the Cat can, too, just as well. Look at the record. I don't care what team it is, even if it has a Seaver or a Sutton, I'd rather have Hunter. But the Blue Boy will do. And if he doesn't, it will be Hunter's turn and that will be that."

Blue got by. He blanked the Dodgers for five innings. He gave up two runs in the sixth. Odom took over in the seventh to protect a 2–2 tie. In the home half, Rudi hit a home run off of Mike Marshall, relieving Sutton. Series MVP Fingers took over in the eighth to protect the 3–2 lead and finished the Dodgers with the help of the last of several spectacular plays afield by Green.

The A's had become the only team outside the old Yankees to win three World Series in succession. And had picked up another $25,000 paycheck in the process.

They celebrated, but like businessmen, not boys. Finley strutted around, shaking hands, hogging the spotlight. "He held his hand out, you had to do something with it," one of the players said laughingly. He held his hand out to Hunter, who shook it. Hunter went to the platform that had been erected in the clubhouse for television and he and Bando and Campaneris accepted the title trophy on behalf of all the A's from commissioner Kuhn. At the request of Finley, Jackson jumped up, joined in, and sprayed the commissioner with champagne.

Still blinking from the bright lights, a disheveled Jim Hunter sat on his stool in front of his locker. He did not seem happy, but he smiled and said he was happy. "I feel a lot of pride in my team," he said. It was pointed out he had played a prominent part in it. "I'm proud of that," he said. It was pointed out that it might not be his team much longer. "I don't want to talk about that," he said. He sighed.

He looked around at the A's, an outrageous group of rebels, but a great team, his team for the last time. He sighed and seemed wistful. He bent over, his head hung and his expression hidden. After a while, he straightened up, stripped off his green and gold uniform, and got ready to go home to North Carolina.

10

When baseball's bigwigs began trying to catch Catfish Hunter, the free-agent pitcher, they first tried to bait the hook with friendships, dispatching personal pals to talk to him.

The first thing Cleveland general manager Phil Seghi did was send Hunter's North Carolina neighbor, Gaylord Perry, on an advance visit to his fellow member in the fraternity of pitchers.

Having himself just signed for $150,000 a year for the next two years, Perry departed Cleveland and returned to his Williamston farm by way of Ahoskie, where he met with Hunter two days ahead of the Indians' official raiding party of Seghi and operating chief Ted Bonda.

"I don't know how much good, if any, I did, but I tried hard," reported Perry. "I told him we have a good young team that could win the pennant next season with just another good starting pitcher—a starting pitcher like Catfish.

"And I also told him he could be the Number One guy, the ace of our staff, if he'd join me in Cleveland," the Indian ace admitted.

"And I said we're both country boys and he wouldn't like the hustle and bustle of a real big city any more than I would. I said Cleveland is a better place to play ball than, say, New York."

And what did the Catfish say?

"He indicated that his decision would be based on what club offers him the best deal," Perry reported.

"I said I couldn't blame him for that." Gaylord grinned.

What representatives of some teams said and what they offered Hunter has been shrouded in secrecy, but behind-the-scenes research with some who were there and were willing to confide developments reveals a lot of what took place behind closed doors.

Cleveland's Perry was not the only representative of a team to talk against New York or, for that matter, one or two other towns. "God, Jim, your wife wouldn't even dare to go to the grocery store in that jungle up there," one suggested.

"You never know who your neighbors will be in that town," pointed out another. "Your kids wouldn't be safe in those schools." Broad hints demeaning blacks and Latins were laid on Hunter, a Southerner who never has been prone to prejudice.

He spoke to Clyde Kluttz, the Yankee scout about New York. "I hated it too at first," admitted Kluttz. "It's not the kind of life we're used to. But you get used to it. You can afford to live any way you want to live. There are nice places to live there, too. In the suburbs.

"If Tom Seaver and Mickey Mantle could adjust, you can.

"People are people. You've got good ones and bad ones. You pick your own friends, anyway. A player lives a private sort of life, anyway. Life in New York has its disadvantages. It also has its advantages. It has a lot to offer."

Turned off by the insensitive slurs directed at the big town by rival bidders, Hunter's feelings about life in New York were eased by Kluttz's comments.

On the surface one of the least prominent persons involved in the proceedings, Kluttz really was a key figure.

In retrospect, it appears that what was destined to be one of the most memorable moments in baseball history, "The Fifteen-Day Fishing Expedition for Catfish Hunter," was most influenced by one of the game's least memorable former players and one of the least notable participants in the proceedings, one Clyde Franklin Kluttz.

As the preliminary planning concluded and the real bidding began in earnest, this apparently minor representative of the New York Yankees skipped through shadows, far from the spotlight, yet by the time his club made the catch it appeared he more than all of the more monied and prominent personalities had played the pivotal role.

A native of North Carolina, Clyde Kluttz was born in Rockwell and still makes his home in nearby Salisbury. He had spent thirty-seven of his fifty-seven years in baseball, many of them in the low minors where he rode buses to games, hung his clothes on hooks, and dined afterward on hamburgers. He spent nine years in the majors, but never made more than $10,500 a season.

A clever catcher and capable hitter, he came out of Catawba College to sign a pro contract with the St. Louis Cardinals. They promised him bonuses of a bird dog and a shotgun, but he got neither. And they never brought him up to the big leagues, either. After he led the Pacific Coast League in hitting in 1941, the Boston Braves drafted him.

He came up to the National League in 1942. In his fourth season with the Braves they traded him to the New York Giants. The next season the Giants traded him to the St. Louis Cardinals. Finally with the Cardinals, he sat on the bench while Joe Garagiola and Del Rice caught the 1946 World Series against the Boston Red Sox. Clyde didn't get into a game. His winner's share was $3,642.

It was the only winner he had ever played with, and none of his teams ever gave him 100 games a season, though he hit .300 twice and compiled a respectable career average of .268.

The next season he passed on to the Pittsburgh Pirates. A couple of seasons later he passed out of the National League and into the American League with the old St. Louis Browns. Early on, he went on to the Washington Senators. He concluded his career in Washington in 1952.

"I was known for my name, but I never was a big name," said Clyde Kluttz, whose name made him the butt of many jokes. Apparently, no one ever believed a "Clyde Kluttz" could catch competently, though he hung on a long time at a time when big league jobs were scarce.

After that he managed here, coached there, scouted here and there. He scouted for Charlie Finley's A's when they were in Kansas City. Covering the Southeast in general and his home state of North Carolina in particular, Kluttz heard about the pitching prospect at Perquimans High in Hertford, one Jimmy Hunter.

Clyde Kluttz spent a lot of afternoons watching Hunter hurl high school games and a lot of evenings visiting with Hunter and his family and occasionally having dinner with them, discussing Jim's potential for a career in professional baseball. They took a liking to him and felt they could trust him.

Kluttz brought Mr. Finley in to talk to the lad and Charlie, a supersalesman, charmed Jim and his parents. Finley authorized Kluttz to go high to sign him.

When Hunter was hurt in a hunting accident, Kluttz pleaded that the youngster still should be signed. Finley went along with him. While other interested teams were backing out, Kluttz signed Jim for the A's for a $50,000 bonus.

A friendship was formed which remained firm in the ten years following, even after Kluttz left Finley's employ in a dispute in which he was refused a brief bit of active on-the-field duty as a coach to qualify as a 10-year man for higher pension payments.

Most of Finley's employees leave him sooner or later over one dispute or another. Kluttz and Hunter, Piedmont Mountain pals, still visited each other often and hunted together through the long winters when they both were back home and baseball was behind them for a few months.

Although by then a director of major league and special assignment scouting for the Yankees, Kluttz was one of the first people Hunter contacted when he was deciding to sue the A's for his freedom. He said he hated to do it. Unselfishly, Kluttz suggested Jimmy ask Finley for a $200,000 bonus and $200,000 a year salary on a long-term contract to drop his action and rejoin his team. Hunter took his advice

Celebrating Series success, Catfish Hunter douses ducking
Rollie Fingers with champagne.

Catfish tells the media about winning final play-off game.

and asked it of Charlie. Finley flatly refused. Hunter determined to pursue his lawsuit.

Finley reminded Hunter of a $150,000 loan he had made Hunter in 1970 to purchase a 500-acre farm. Hunter reminded Finley that so much pressure had been brought to bear for repayment of the loan long before it was due that Catfish's pitching had suffered and in anger he had sold off 400 acres to pay off the loan, now lived on the 100 original acres, and therefore needed a lot more money to buy back the 400 acres he still wanted.

He remembered, but did not remind Finley, that when Vida Blue was burning up the league a few years earlier, Hunter himself was headed for his first big year, yet was rudely shoved aside at times so Blue could pitch out of turn before the big-money home crowds. Hunter remembered and he still hurt a little and it helped him to decide to depart his winning team.

It was strange, but now the biggest-money deal in baseball history was brewing around one of its best players, but not one of its greatest gate attractions, a fellow whose nickname was the most colorful thing about him, and one who had none of the chemical magnetism of a Vida Blue or Nolan Ryan.

When the Yankees joined the hunt for Hunter, they had memories, too. They remembered how only the year before, Dick Williams had apparently been permitted to resign as A's manager to become the Yankee manager by Finley, only to have Charlie turn around and block the move in one of his contrary moments, until they had to hire another manager, Bill Virdon. They remembered how they were in the pennant race until the end, when they lost it, and thought Williams might have won for them.

Commissioner Bowie Kuhn had suspended their owner, George Steinbrenner, for his conduct off the field. Bowie Kuhn really didn't want an auction of a top player that would take him from his "contracted" team to another team without compensation to the original team. But the court ruling was that he no longer was contracted. He was freed, forcing Kuhn's hand. Kuhn had to accept open bidding. And he could not stop the Yankees from bidding.

So it was in several ways more than the desire to add a top player to their team that motivated the Yankees. If they did, these other considerations would make victory in this off-the-field big-game hunt all the sweeter.

The Yankees put more than money into their bid. The veteran baseball man, Gabe Paul, now president of the Yankees, had begun swiftly to rebuild what once was the finest of franchises. In October he had dealt disappointing Bobby Murcer, who had turned out not to be the "new Mickey Mantle," to San Francisco for "the new Willie Mays," Bobby Bonds. Now, in December, he had the chance to add the top pitcher in the game.

The Mets had risen from rags to riches, catching and surpassing the fabled Yankees, not only on the field, but in the hearts of New York fans. Forced to share Shea Stadium until Yankee Stadium was rebuilt in a desparate effort to enhance their appeal, the Yankees now were determined to outbid the Mets and everyone else for Catfish Hunter.

Mayor Abe Beame sent Hunter a personal letter saying how much everyone in New York would like to have Hunter in that city. Seeking the same sort of personal touch other teams used, the Yankees had another former A's teammate, Curt Blefray, write to Hunter about the good life in the suburbs of New York City—in New Jersey, for example, or Westchester, or Long Island, or Connecticut. "I wrote him a single-spaced, three-page letter," says Blefray, now a sheriff's officer in New Jersey.

At his own expense, Thurman Munson telephoned the Catfish several times. "You're the kind of pitcher I'd sure like to catch," the catcher said.

And, most effective of all, the Yankees sent their special assignment scout, Clyde Kluttz, to help them bag the Catfish, his old friend. Clyde drove the 300 miles from his home in Salisbury to Hunter's home in Hertford and visited Jimmy. They had dinner at Hunter's house, served by his wife, Helen, and then they walked and talked in the woods.

Then Kluttz went, not to Ahoskie, near the Cherry offices, but to a motel 12 miles from Hunter's home. While others conferred with Hunter and his group in Ahoskie, Kluttz killed the days reading newspapers and watching television in his room near Hertford.

After Hunter's days were done and he drove home in his Ford pickup, Kluttz either called him or went over to chat with him. Hunter welcomed his interest. "I like him and I trust him," Hunter says. "I felt he was as much on my side as he was on the side of his team. I could talk to him."

"I never tried to high-pressure Jimmy. I never said my job was on the line or anything like that. It wasn't. I wanted to help my team, but I wanted to help him, too," Kluttz says.

"It was no secret I wanted him to go with the Yankees. That was understood. We went on from there. If another team offered him a better deal, he had to consider it, of course."

No one did, until the very end. But then no one, not the Yankees and not anyone else, put down exact details of their bid until the very end. There was a lot of talk of what Hunter wanted and what the others wanted to give him, but not much on paper.

Right from the start the Yankees made it clear they were ready to bid with the best of the offers.

The only times Kluttz went to Ahoskie was when he picked up Gabe Paul and the Yankee party at the airport and drove them to the meetings before bringing them back to the airport.

At all other times he stayed close to Hunter's house, visited him whenever he could, and waited. "It was a long wait. A man could grow old on a wait of a couple of weeks like that," the graying baseball veteran confesses, smiling.

Some teams telephoned in their offers, but most teams visited Ahoskie to present their pitches in person. Several came a couple of times. Only the Yankees came three times. All along, the Yankees thought they'd land the pitcher, until the last time.

"We thought he wanted to go with us. We thought he would go with us," Gabe Paul admits. "When I left for the last trip to North Carolina just a few days before the end of the year and the end of the bidding, I believed I would return with him. I was so sure I had a press conference planned for our offices on New Year's Eve.

"But when he didn't say yes to the sort of program we spoke about in that last meeting, I got the sinking feeling that we'd lost him. I figured one or two teams had offered him so much money neither we nor anyone else in our right minds would match it. I sensed his lawyers wanted him to go for the dough, more than anything else.

"I didn't call off the press conference, and when I said good-bye to Clyde Kluttz I told him to wait it out, but I was worried all the way back on the plane flight," Paul admits.

But Clyde Kluttz waited it out.

11

The A's, Astros, Orioles, Giants, Cubs, and White Sox had bowed out of the bidding for Catfish Hunter early on in the negotiations. Neither the Cardinals nor Mets were willing to go on when the price reached $2,000,000. The Angels and Twins dropped out at about this level. The Rangers, Braves and Expos fell out at $2,500,000. The Phils fell out just a little past that point.

At Christmastime, the Pirates, Reds, Dodgers, Padres, Red Sox, Royals, and Yankees remained in the running.

There are those who will say Christmas came a little late for the Hunters that year of 1974. Actually, it fell on Tuesday. Starting on Sunday, Catfish insisted on a break in the negotiations. Sunday morning the Hunter family went to church, where Helen Hunter sings in the choir. Then the family retired to their farmhouse to rest.

The day after Christmas, Pirate scout George Pratt sat in the lobby of the Tomahawk Motel talking to Dutch Overton, the assistant principal of Ahoskie High.

"Time really flies all right," Pratt was saying. "It wasn't ten, maybe twelve years ago I was assistant baseball coach over at Hertford where Jim was playing. We was always short of money and most times I'd wind up umpiring our games behind the plate. They'd always say, 'No wonder Jimmy wins—he brings his own umpire.'"

Overton laughed and allowed as how there was more to it than that.

Someone asked Pratt about his ring. It was a World Series ring the Pirates had presented him and he showed it proudly. He, himself, never had made the majors as a player. He had heart trouble and was scouting for the Pirates. He was the sort of down-home sort North Carolinians liked and had been brought in to take a fatherly approach to Catfish, but he was not optimistic.

"Say, ya'all talk with 'em in the morning?" he was asked.

"Us in the morning, Cincinnati in the afternoon," he said.

"Who's going to win 'im?" he was asked.

"The Yankees," he said. "Clyde Kluttz is their top scout and he and Jim go hunting together all the time. Jim could make an awful lot of extra money in New York, don't forget that. And the Yankees can start winning pennants again if they get him. If I had to bet on it, I'd say the Yankees."

That was the talk by then, but some didn't want to believe it, and in truth it wasn't entirely true. The Yankees had made offers, which had passed the $3,000,000 level, in two trips to Ahoskie and Hunter liked other parts of the package that went with joining them, but he'd had to tell Kluttz he was still undecided.

Kansas City's Royals had suggested they'd go higher, while San Diego's Padres had said they'd go higher yet and Catfish's lawyers were lobbying for the top figure. One or two other clubs were hinting they weren't finished yet, too. Some infighting was going on between Catfish and his counsel.

The Pirate party came in and went out at the $2,800,000 figure. They stretched their limit as far as they were willing to go before surrendering. General manager Joe Brown said, "We'd have liked to have had him. With our hitting, he might have made us unbeatable. But you get no guarantees. And you can't risk the entire financial structure of your operation to bet on one pitcher."

The Reds came to talk more than anything else. They wanted to know what was happening. They did not want to tie themselves to the sort of contract for Hunter that was developing, but they wanted to make sure others in their league, especially the Dodgers, did not.

When the Pirates dropped out, the Dodgers dropped out. When the Dodgers dropped out, the Reds dropped out.

The Reds and Dodgers stalled to make sure the other did not make a bid for Hunter they might have to outbid. They were worried about the competition within their own division mainly. But they were also worried a bit about competition from the other divisions they might have to oppose in the play-offs so they hung in until the Mets, Phils, and finally the Pirates pulled out.

This left only San Diego from the National League in the running and even Catfish Hunter could not put the Padres in the pennant race. So, stealing looks back over their shoulders to make sure a rival was not sneaking back into contention, the Pirates, Reds, and Dodgers departed the contention.

Boston bowed out at $3,000,000. General manager O'Connell commented, "We dropped out of the bidding when the terms become so high that we didn't think them fair to the rest of our team." However, other Red Sox sources confide that the club was prepared to go to $4,000,000, but were discouraged after talks with Hunter, which led them to believe he did not really want to pitch in their tiny park.

A spokesman for the Montreal Expos said general manager Fanning's final bid had been a firm offer of between $3,000,000 and $4,000,000, but that Hunter was worried about the ball park there and was not sure he wanted to set up residence in cold Canada, far from his South.

Montreal's Fanning and Atlanta's general manger Robinson still spoke as though they were in the running. Robinson said, "Hunter's attorneys have notified twenty of the twenty-four teams, saying they are no longer in the picture. We were not one of those so notified. So, as far as we know now, we still have a good chance."

Carlton Cherry said, "If an individual club is willing to say it is in the running, we will say they are. You can say we confirm it. I wish I could tell you the names of the clubs that are still in the running, but I don't feel at liberty to do so. We do anticipate we will be able to announce whom he will sign with shortly."

Hunter was applying pressure to them. They were near the end of the year now and Catfish wanted to end the embarrassment and sign so he could discontinue commuting daily to Ahoskie, know whom he was going to be with the following season, and slip back into the shadows to resume his hunting and winter rest.

By now the financial figures being tossed around were beginning to seem unreal to all concerned. When you get to talking a lot about $3,000,000 and $4,000,000 after a while the amounts lose their real significance and there doesn't seem to be much difference between them, though the reality is that $1,000,000 certainly is significant.

It's like being in Las Vegas a while and watching people pitch change into the slot machines and throw dollars and chips across the tables, and starting to do so yourself. Money seems to lose its meaning. It's not the same there as it is at home when you're writing out checks to pay the bills and seeing the bank account shrink.

It wasn't the same in Ahoskie at that conference table as it was elsewhere.

The big-business men wanted to wrap it up, too, because on both sides it would be beneficial to sign before the end of one year so the investment and taxes could be spread over that year and the next, over two years instead of one. By the thirtieth, two days before the end of the year, everyone was wearing down and getting down to what they had decided would be their final bids.

And the fact was that the contenders for Catfish's contract had been reduced to four teams, and the four teams were Cleveland, Kansas City, San Diego, and New York's Yankees, no matter what anyone else thought or said.

Hunter's lawyers weren't going to embarrass anyone who said they were still in it by saying they were not. For all the attorneys knew, one of them would yet pop up with the best bid yet. But time was running out and the contenders could not go much higher.

Cleveland's Bonda and Seghi flew in for a second time to confirm the Indians' last offer, which still stood at terms amounting to $3,800,000.

They were the most surprising team remaining in contention, but had just hired the major league's first black manager, Frank Robinson, and were embarking on a program to rebuild baseball interest in the Ohio city. The Indians had a few things going for them, but not what New York had. They had to outbid others on the money end. They did not.

Owner Ewing Kauffman of the Kansas City Royals personally accompanied general manager Joe Burke to Ahoskie to bid for Hunter. They had worked out a substantial bid which included some unusual features, such as a long-range insurance program to benefit not only the Catfish, but his wife and children. Financially it figured out to around $4,000,000 the last time it was laid on the table. Kauffman was confident.

Aside from not being on the East Coast, the K.C. club represented many of the things Hunter wanted in his new team, but he was wary of Kauffman, who was an extravagant sort of man who seemed to some a sort of Finley, though not as far out. However, Hunter's attorneys were sympathetic to the Royals' offer and wanted Jim to consider it seriously.

On Monday the thirtieth, president Buzzy Bavasi of the Padres, his son, vice-president and general manager, Peter Bavasi, and vice-president and secretary Don Lubin got together in a conference call with Carlton Cherry, Flythe, and Hunter, which lasted from 5 to 5:45 P.M. At the deadline, they discussed for one last time terms of the contract offered by Ray Kroc's San Diego entry.

San Diego did not represent many of the things Hunter wanted in a town and a team, but their offer represented many of the things his attorneys wanted. It was pegged at past $4,000,000. A member of the organization privately put it at $4,400,000, but some say the Padres were prepared to go higher. Kroc made it clear he would top any other offer by a good bit.

The Cherry team wanted Hunter to take it.

Hunter wasn't so sure he should. He drove home thinking about it. Meanwhile, Kluttz had taken Gabe Paul and the Yankee attorney to the airport and put them on the plane back to the big city. All the way there they talked about where they could add a nickel here, a dime there, to their offer. They thought Hunter wanted to go with them, but they didn't have his name on the line yet.

As soon as he returned to the motel, Kluttz called the Catfish one more time. He had called him or seen him every evening for two weeks and at this point he wasn't going to stop, though he was worried he was making a nuisance of himself. However, Jim said, "I'm glad you called. I've got to talk to you one more time." He was tired. He didn't want to talk any more that night. But could Clyde meet him for breakfast the next morning? Clyde could.

On the morning of the thirty-first, Catfish and Clyde met at a restaurant, ate, and talked. The Catfish confessed he was confused by then by all the terms that had been tossed at him. He wanted to go with Clyde's team, but they had to come close to the other top offers. Finally, then, what did the Yankee offer come down to?

He'd write it out, Kluttz said. He picked up a paper napkin, pulled a pen out of his pocket, and in a restaurant surrounded by strangers, this scout who really knew nothing about big business jotted down on a napkin the terms of the fattest deal in baseball history.

He wrote down $1,000,000 for a bonus, $1,000,000 life insurance for the player, $500,000 for a retirement pension program over ten years, and $200,000 in the desired attorneys' fees. After debating terms, the Yankee brass had rounded each part of the program into nice round figures.

"Is that your offer?" Hunter asked.

"Yes, Jimmy, that's it. And it's our final offer." Clyde sighed.

"Don't leave town. I'll get with you in an hour," Hunter said.

Clyde wasn't going anywhere. He waited while Hunter went to talk to his attorneys. He told them this was what he wanted. They pointed out others offered more. Hunter said this one came close enough, considering that it was the Yankees.

Carlton Cherry sighed and said for Jimmy to get Kluttz. Clyde came in nervously. Cherry waved the napkin. "I don't agree with all this," he admitted, "but Jimmy insists on picking his own club. Is this the offer, then?" he asked Kluttz.

"Yes," Kluttz said.

"Then he's a Yankee," Cherry said.

Tears came to Clyde's eyes. He admitted it later. Catfish grinned broadly and banged his old hunting buddy on the back.

They acted as though a bloody war had ended.

12

It was 12:30 in the afternoon of Tuesday, the thirty-first of December, when the Yankees landed the prize catch, Catfish Hunter, for which 22 other big league baseball teams had been angling, but it was a few minutes later before the official family found out in New York.

After telling Yankee scout Clyde Kluttz that their client, Hunter, had decided on the New York team, J. Carlton Cherry added that there were some loose ends that had to be tied together and put on paper.

Did he think the Yankees could work these out with them that day?

Kluttz said of course, he was sure they could, though, of course, he really did not know.

"Then you better call." Cherry smiled.

Clyde guessed as to how he better do that little thing.

He called Gabe Paul, who let out a holler.

The 15-day expedition, which had been officially launched on the sixteenth of December, had ended.

There were still some details to be decided and incorporated into a contract.

Could they do it right away? Kluttz asked Paul.

"We'll do it today," Paul said. "Can Jim and his attorneys come to New York for a press conference that very night?"

Kluttz asked the Hunter party. They said they could, if they could make connections.

Told this, Paul told them he'd send a plane for them right away. They could iron out the details on the plane and in New York, Paul said. Cherry agreed.

The press conference still was on call. Now it was confirmed for 8:15 that night.

Paul called Ed Greenwald, also a Yankee partner and the team lawyer, in Cleveland. Ed agreed to charter a jet, fly to Norfolk, pick up the Hunter party, and fly to New York with them, while working out details of the contract.

He started to write out the contract in longhand on a yellow legal pad while the plane flew him south. The Hunter party drove to Norfolk and met the jet. On their way to New York, the attorneys conferred and Greenwald continued to scribble until he had filled 10 pages.

The scrawl was such that Greenwald joked, "I'm the only one who can read it."

Hunter and Kluttz sat apart, talking hunting and farming and North Carolina, two native Tar Heels on their way to the Big City to do a little business.

On arrival in New York, they were hustled by limousine to the Yankee offices where the attorneys gathered with Paul and other advisers to tie up all those loose ends.

Hunter was given approval rights to any future trade, for example. And the Yankees agreed to cover costs of any court cases brought by Finley.

The bonus was to be paid in $100,000 increments —$100,000 now and $100,000 a year for nine more years. They would take $50,000 a year from his $200,000 a year salary and defer it for 10 years. The retirement plan would be spread out to $50,000 a year for 10 years. The $1,000,000 life insurance program would provide $50,000 a year later.

What about insurance for Hunter's children? Couldn't something be worked out there? It could. There would be $25,000 insurance provided each of his two sons. The deal now amounted to $3,750,000 in eventual benefits for Hunter.

Such deals sometimes never seem to be done.

Writers, photographers, broadcasters, and cameramen, many of them having left New Year's Eve parties, filled the

Yankees' offices as the conference time of 8:15 came and went.

A Yankee spokesman said, "We may have a bigger announcement than you think. We may announce we couldn't get together, and the deal is off." Everyone laughed.

What deal? The conference had been called, but no announcement had been made as to the subject matter. Oh, everyone knew. By then the speculation had spread across the country: The Yankees had called a New Year's Eve press conference. Clearly, it could be for no other reason than to announce the signing of Catfish Hunter.

Outside, snow was falling. The city was festive, full of parties. At 8:30 the signing took place behind closed doors. Two minutes later, a $6.25 Yankee cap having been placed on his head, long-haired, mustachioed Catfish Hunter emerged with the group to the cheers of the convened newsmen.

He sat down in front of a battery of microphones and lights. On his right was Greenwald. On his left were Paul and Kluttz. Hunter's four attorneys stood behind them. Paul made the announcement: The Yankees were proud to announce the signing of James "Catfish" Hunter.

His manager, Bill Virdon, was on hand, beaming, presuming a pennant had been handed him.

Paul also mentioned George Steinbrenner, who was not on hand, barred by Bowie Kuhn.

"How much money was involved?" he was asked.

"That's confidential, of course." He smiled.

"When was the deal concluded?"

"A few minutes ago. Not until a few minutes ago, really." He laughed.

"When did you shake hands on the deal?"

"We haven't yet." Catfish smiled.

They shook hands, then, smiling, as cameras rolled and flashbulbs popped.

It was Catfish's turn. He was wearing blue slacks and a blue, long-sleeved sweater-shirt, and that cap with the "NY" on the front of it.

Christmas, 1974, came with a rich gift of cash and security for Jim Hunter, his wife, Helen, and their two children, Kimberly and Todd.

Louis Requena and the New York Yankees

His attorneys stand behind him as Catfish announces his signing with the New York Yankees during the New Year's Eve (1975) press conference.

"How much money?" he was asked.

"I don't know." He smiled. "But maybe when I get through playing, I can sit down and count it."

"Two million? Three million?" The questioners persisted.

"Ten million." Catfish grinned.

Was he satisfied?

"I am delighted or I wouldn't be here."

Everybody laughed.

"I always wanted to play in New York. I always wanted to be a Yankee," the Southerner said. "I remember I used to get chills just walking into Yankee Stadium. I think every ballplayer has felt that in his heart. Now there's going to be a new Yankee Stadium. With a natural grass surface. I'll be proud to be a part of it. All that great tradition . . ."

So the ghosts of Ruth, Gehrig, DiMaggio, and Mantle were in the room, too, along with Clyde Kluttz.

When the Yankees bought Babe Ruth from Boston, he cost them $125,000. Clyde Kluttz cost even less.

"I don't think I would have signed with the Yankees if anybody but Clyde had contacted me for them," confessed the Catfish, despite the fact that it contradicted what he had just said about the pull of the team, its arena, and its history.

"Clyde signed me for the A's the first time about ten years ago. Clyde never lied to me about anything then and I knew he wouldn't lie to me now. I felt I could trust him, which is important in a complicated deal like this one. And my friendship with him meant a lot to me, too," Catfish said.

Clyde Kluttz beamed. He had brought his team this star, though there was not a nickel in the contract for him.

Looking worn-out by now, the old catcher commented, "My desire to get him this time wasn't any different than it was when I signed him the last time. If he'd signed with another team it wouldn't have changed a thing between us. He's the kind of person you'd want as a son. Especially"—Kluttz laughed—"now that he's got all that money."

Which brought laughter.

Tom Cherry said, "Money was no object in the end. It was purely and simply a matter of personal preference by Jimmy."

If, Jimmy was asked, the Yankees really were the team he wanted all along, why had he bothered to entertain other offers? Were others really in the running?

"That's for me to know and you to find out," Hunter said with a smile.

Carlton Cherry confided that it really wasn't a bad way to bargain for better terms.

Tom Flythe was asked, "Is it fair to call Catfish a millionaire now?"

"It's fair to call him a multimillionaire." The lawyer smiled.

The multimillionaire was handed a $13.21 fishing pole by Neal Walsh, deputy commissioner of special events for Mayor Abe Beame and the City of New York. It was a gift, and symbolic of the catch the town had made.

Someone had scoured the city for an open sporting goods store to purchase the pole in the late hours of this holiday evening. Catfish thanked the mayor's representative and said he'd do his best to put the Yankees back on top.

Did he feel he faced special pressures to produce a pennant because of his big contract? he was asked.

"This is still a team game," Hunter observed. "All I can do is my share. I'll do my best."

Gabe Paul said, "If he didn't have as much pride as he has, we wouldn't have given him a five-year contract."

The contract was for five years, then?

"Five years," Paul admitted, sighing. "He's a proud person and an exceptional pitcher. He pitched as well after he planned to leave the A's as before. I'm sure he'd pitch as well for us if he wasn't being paid a penny as he will for the money he will make."

"He's a smart pitcher," Yankee manager Bill Virdon said. "He has good physical tools, but more important he has a good mind and knows how to pitch. You don't run as great a risk paying a lot for a pitcher like this as you do for one who depends strictly on physical things.

"He could help us to a pennant, but you can't count on anything like that. Other players are involved. He'll help us, that's all I can count on. There's not much you can count on in this sport. You never know what will happen," Virdon concluded wistfully.

"Will the other players resent the sort of money Hunter was going to make?"

"I don't think so," Virdon said. "I think they all wish they were in his position. I think they all know he can put money in their pockets. They all want to win. They know he can help us win. If we don't win, we're all in trouble, Jim Hunter or no Jim Hunter," Virdon added.

Jim Hunter was feeling the heat. He was worn out and wanted to get home. He hadn't mentioned Charlie Finley and loans that had hurt him and a contract that hadn't been fulfilled and court cases he still might face and all the tumult on the team he had left and all the teammates he had left behind who now would try to win a fourth straight world title without him, and he didn't want to. He didn't want to talk anymore.

One day was left in the deer-hunting season back home and he wanted to take advantage of it. He had told his father before he left he'd be back before dawn the last day to hunt with him and he meant to be there.

Suddenly seeming exhausted, he sighed and said, "It's been a long day. I don't know when I made up my mind to go with the Yankees, but I didn't make a final decision until today. But I think when I left home this morning my wife knew that was the way I was going.

"She said anything I wanted was all right with her.

"It was seven thirty this morning when I left home. It's time to start back," he said.

He and his attorneys headed beyond the gaudy neon lights of the big town to the airport to make National Airlines flight 75 at ten to ten, bound for Norfolk.

New Yankee star Jim Hunter hurls one.

It was around midnight when they landed in Norfolk. Catfish drove home through the dark night, through the tree-thick countryside.

The next day Phil Wrigley, the owner of the Cubs, sent a statement to the three daily newspapers remaining in Chicago. In part it said, "Things now seem to be out of hand. The offers represent in our opinion more money than the average fan will pay to see a whole team, much less one player.

"In a time of recession, it does not make much sense. . . . The present circumstances have resulted in a frenzied action which has placed everything out of perspective. . . .

"Much as the Cubs would like to have Jim Hunter, they do not intend to become involved in a situation which, according to news reports, is, in our opinion, unrealistic."

The heir to the chewing gum fortune, the progressive-thinking recluse who seldom has even been seen by any of his players and who remains the only owner who has denied his fans lights for night games so they can see their team after working hours, did not seem aware the auction was over.

Ray Kroc knew it was over. The fast-food king complained angrily that his offers had been used by Hunter's group to boost the bidding for the pitcher's services. "He was going to sign with the Yankees from day one," Kroc charged.

"I feel we've been used. I'm a bad loser.

"He talked about where his family would like to live. He said his wife had always had a very high regard for San Diego: it was clean and homey looking, and that's the kind of place she liked.

"When he said it looked like he was going to go with the Yankees, we said to him, 'If it's strictly money, we don't want to let a few dollars stand in the way.'

"Then he had the gall to say, 'Well, after you get a certain amount, it doesn't make much difference whether you get more or not.'

"All of a sudden, money is not really that important.

"Then he makes a statement when it's all over that he's been a Yankee lover all his life and he wants to live and play in New York."

Kroc threw up his hands in disgust.

Well, when four million dollars isn't enough to purchase a player, what is a man to think?

When a man suggests he'd rather live in New York than in San Diego, where has reason gone?

Well, maybe it was just as well it was over. Going to the golden arches, a customer might no longer have been able to get a hamburger, fries, a shake, and change for a buck if he'd have had to chip in on Catfish's contract.

In Kansas City, Ewing Kauffman sighed and said, "I'm sorry we lost, but I'm glad it's over."

The only one who didn't feel it was over, finally, was Charles Oscar Finley. In Oakland, Charlie O said, "It's not over yet. We'll carry our case to the highest courts. We want to bring him back where he belongs."

But by then, the very rich Jimmy Hunter was in the woods hunting with his old man.

13

Returning in a relaxed mood to the plane that waited to take them back to the South from.New York, a bit heady from the headlines they had just made, one of Jim Hunter's attorneys said to another one, "I'll betcha a buck the stewardess recognizes Jim and knows who he is."

"It's a bet," the second one said.

The second one won. The stewardess gave no indication she recognized the mustachioed young man wearing the NY baseball cap. Asked if she knew who he was, she said she did not. Told who he was, she shrugged and said she wasn't a sports fan. Hunter smiled.

On landing in Norfolk just before midnight, the attorneys went to a car rental counter. Anxious to get his buck back, the first attorney suggested a new bet based on the girl behind the counter recognizing Jim. The second one took the bet and won again.

Having arrived back home at 3 in the morning, Jim Hunter had rolled out before 7 to join his father in a hunt for their first deer of the season on the last day of the deer-hunting season. Three of Jim's four brothers and a few friends went along also.

A reporter arriving at the Hunter home in Hertford about 9 was told by Helen that Jim was long gone. "He went to the big woods, but I don't know just where that is," admitted Mrs. Hunter.

"But you won't have any trouble spotting him. He's in a silver pickup truck with little wheels that sit up real high," she added.

However, he had trouble. He drove more than 100 miles

over one dirt road after another in pursuit of the pitcher, passing a taxicab along the way.

Taxicab? Out of place on these back roads, it was, it turned out, loaded with big-city television cameramen seeking to tape the player's first day as a multimillionaire.

Finally, the reporter asked some other hunters how he might find the Catfish. Well, he was told, he was not the Catfish to them, he was "Silver Bullet."

That's the code name he used on the citizen-band radio sets most of them used in their cars and trucks to keep up contact with others.

"Come in, Silver Bullet, come in," radioed one helpful hunter.

"This is Silver Bullet," came the reply.

"There's a fellow here who wants to see you for a few minutes," Silver Bullet was told.

Silver Bullet said where he was, describing a part of the forest a few miles away.

The reporter found him. Introducing himself, he asked Silver Bullet if he'd had any luck.

"No, not yet," Silver Bullet admitted, "but I hope I get a buck before the day is over."

The reporter mentioned that he'd seen a deer on his way there. Before he could explain that it was only a doe, or begin to ask him about baseball or multimillion-dollar contracts, Silver Bullet was asking excitedly, "Where, where, where?"

As the reporter pointed in the direction from which he'd come, Silver Bullet was sliding back behind the steering wheel of his pickup truck.

"There's a taxicab full of cameramen looking for you," the reporter shouted.

"Well, they ain't gonna find me," Silver Bullet shouted back as he roared away in search of that elusive buck.

However, he returned home empty-handed that night. "As usual, I didn't get anything. I haven't gotten anything this year," he said. "Deer, that is," he added with a smile.

He had gotten a few of some other kind of bucks, but was

bound and determined that was not going to alter him or his life-style. "I'm the same person I always was. Just richer, I guess." And he grinned.

"A lot of people think I demanded a lot of money. I didn't," Hunter said. "I never demanded any kind of money. I just said I wanted security for my wife and my children and for when I got out of baseball. The owners went from there. They made their proposals. When they asked us, we told them what sort of money was being proposed. It tended to mount up."

Coming to call a day or two later, a reporter was told Jim was outside "mowing the ditches."

Mowing the ditches?

"The grass in and around the ditches, so we can spot the snakes that get in them," Helen Hunter explained.

Wearing a heavy brown jacket, an orange windbreaker, and a green hunting cap while he worked, Jim said, "I'm gonna come back here to live the rest of my life after baseball is behind me, so I might as well get used to the work again."

He, Helen, and their children, Todd, five years old, and Kimberly, 18 months old, live with 23 hunting dogs—beagles and hounds—and 200 head of Black Angus cattle on the original 100-acre spread outside of Hertford, which he purchased with a $150,000 loan from Charlie Finley five years earlier.

Actually, it is 113 acres. And on it they had built a $100,000 red-brick, colonial-ranch home. It has 10 rooms, five of them bedrooms, and spans 5,000 square feet. It has a sewing room, a recreation room, and a playroom.

"It's our only luxury, but we don't live luxurious," Helen Hunter said. Dark-haired and domestic, tiny and pretty, Helen Hunter cooks and cans vegetables they grow themselves.

She said, "I spend most of my time taking care of the house, the children, and Jim. He's easy to take care of. He's not a fussy eater, for example. He doesn't like casseroles. He just likes meat and potatoes. I'm a lot like that, too. My favorite is any kind of hamburger dish. His favorite is Swiss steak. I'll probably fix him some to celebrate."

She was asked about the incredible contract her husband had signed. "It's security, I suppose." She sighed. "But the idea of that kind of money really is hard to grasp. There's nobody around here with that kind of money. Neither Jim nor I had much money when we were growing up.

"Even now I find myself looking at prices and thinking how awful they are. I could make a lot of things cheaper, myself. I like to sew and I like to make things, like the candleholders I made for Christmas.

"Jim still gives his hunting dogs their shots himself, because it's cheaper than going to the vet. I don't think it's in us to throw money around."

She describes herself as the daughter of the best butcher in Edonton, about 15 miles down the road from Hertford. She was one of 11 children, while he, the son of a farmer, was one of 9.

"I never saw Jim until I was in the eighth grade, 'cause we lived in town and he lived out on the farm," she recalls. "We have two schools in Hertford. One goes from the first to the seventh grades, the other, from the eighth through the twelfth grades. That's Perquimans High School. We're in Perquimans County.

"We went to the same high school, but he was two years older than me and two grades ahead of me. He was in his third year of high school and I was in my first year when I saw him on the school bus for the first time. I remember he was talking baseball. He still talks baseball.

"I became a cheerleader, but we didn't talk much until he was a senior and I was a sophomore. He was eighteen and I was sixteen. The school had this Sadie Hawkins Day dance and the girls were supposed to invite the boys. I was too shy to invite him, so he sort of asked me to ask him. I went with him, and we started dating.

"The courtship was just slow and easy. He worked in a filling station after school and after work he'd come over to my house and we'd just sit around. I guess it hasn't changed much since we were married. We were married when he was twenty and I was eighteen. He was already in the major leagues, his second season as a professional player. We sit around and watch TV a lot, rather than go out."

He calls himself a farmboy and kids her by calling her a city girl, but she describes herself as a small-town girl who had difficulty adjusting to the commotion Jim's contract negotiations caused.

"I'm glad it's over. It got a little nerve-racking," she said. "We have a listed number and just everybody was calling. The phone just never seemed to stop ringing. Why didn't I take it off the hook? Oh, we couldn't do that. We're on a party line with Jim's parents and they wouldn't be able to call out.

"But now we are going to get an unlisted number. We hate to do it, but we have to. Our friends will know our number, anyway."

Right from the start of her marriage she had difficulty adjusting to the commotion of her husband's career, even when he was playing in Kansas City and he was not a star.

"I feel the tension. I get nervous when he pitches. I think most players' wives get nervous. You can watch him work, you know. The ups and downs are hard to get used to. Everyone knows how he's doing," she said.

She found California drastically different from the state she knew. "California was so fast-going, I just couldn't get used to it. Everything is slower in North Carolina."

In seasons, through the summer, the Hunters had been renting a house in Walnut Creek, some 45 miles from the Oakland ball park. Teammates Darold Knowles and Paul Lindblad lived with their families on the same street.

"When the team was on the road we used to go out bowling together or to a movie," she said. "I tried playing bridge, but I never did catch on to that."

Now she would have a new house in a new neighborhood in the New York area for the next season. "It scares me some," she said, "but as long as Jim and I and the kids are together, I suppose it'll be all right."

Ahoskie Herald

Jim Hunter works with his hunting dogs.

Playing with son, Todd, and dog, Chief.

She said they looked forward to returning to North Carolina and home every winter, escaping the spotlight and hectic pace of his summers. "Only this winter there has been no escape." She sighed.

"Maybe now that he's signed up we can spend a few quiet evenings at home," she wondered wistfully. "He hasn't been home much. He hasn't had time to play with the kids much. Jim loves his children. Todd loves his father. He loves playing with him. He misses him when he's away.

"Jimmy took Todd hunting with him. Todd loved that. Jimmy loves hunting and fishing. He likes walking in the woods. He likes being with his dogs. I never get involved with the dogs. Jim's brother, Ray, takes care of the dogs when Jim is gone.

"Ray does the farming on Jimmy's land because Jim has been away so much. The land is planted for peanuts and soybeans. We sell what we grow. Jimmy likes farming, but I think it's the farm life he really likes. He likes being at home on the farm. But he'd miss baseball.

"It's hunting and fishing and baseball that Jim loves almost as much as his family," she said.

Jim Hunter said, "Baseball is easy. You train one month, play six months, and you're off for five months. For me that comes at the right time of the year, just when the hunting is good. But when I put on a baseball uniform, I'm one hundred percent. I don't go out to lose. I go out to win. I don't care if it's a cow pasture game.

"I like the life. It's like a dream world for a country boy like me. But sometimes I feel guilty about it. Like things were too easy. After all, a pitcher gets paid a lot of money to work only forty days a year. You've got to be there six or seven months, but you've only got to work forty games or so.

"When I was a boy on a farm in North Carolina I used to load watermelons for twelve hours a day. I could never do that now. I'm too soft from the easy living.

"Now when I think about being a farmer again, I think of being a dude farmer, a gentleman farmer, like Mr. Finley.

"There have been a lot of seasons in baseball when I wasn't paid as much as I should have been paid. I wasn't making as much as others who were doing less. But it was still a lot of money for the work.

"Now I'm making a lot more. And it's too much, really, except that what you do brings in money and it's what they're willing to pay you to do what you do.

"So it's a good life, but it could make you lazy.

"Farm life is really the best way to live. It teaches you how to work, so you work harder when you get a chance to make it. I worked hard to make the most of my chance in baseball. I think a lot of kids today don't know how to work hard.

"I wouldn't trade farm life for anything. On the farm you're your own boss. There's nobody barking at you all the time. In the off-season I run the plow, fish, and hunt coon on into the night.

"It's peaceful walking the woods late at night, following the sounds of the dogs. Some nights I'll walk thirty miles before I realize it.

"I think if I didn't play baseball, I might have been a game warden or something like that, something where I could be in the woods a lot.

"As a farmer, I still help the neighbors with their crops, like we used to do when I was a boy. One year I helped a neighbor spray his peanut crop. When I'm sitting around the clubhouse eating a bag of peanuts, I wonder if I didn't have a hand in growing them. It gives me a good feeling to know maybe I did.

"I've got a commercial for dog food. That's good. I figure I spend more on feeding my dogs than feeding my wife and two kids. Before I left Hertford last February I bought a ton of feed and by the end of May it was gone. It takes three hundred pounds a week to feed 'em. That's at fifteen dollars per hundred pounds.

"I've hunted since I could walk. I was taught to handle a hunting gun before I could throw a baseball. I've learned a lot about hunting dogs. I can tell each of my hounds by the sound of its howl. Everybody's got his own kind of music. A dog's howl is a kind of music to a hunter. Each dog sounds different.

"If I get to do a lot of commercials on TV about dogs, that'll be fine, but I don't want to take up a lot of my free time doing it.

"When I'm getting paid to play baseball, that's the bosses' time. When the baseball season is over, that's my time. I don't want to be going around the United States making appearances all the time, and stuff like that.

"A lot of the A's, they'd go out to banquets and sell themselves in the winter. But hunting and fishing is what I want to do in the winter. I don't have to make money in the winter. In the winter I want to go home and do what I want to do.

"When I go back home in the off-season I seldom go into town so people won't make a fuss over me. I love baseball, but I don't want to talk it all the time. I want to get away from it at times. I don't want to be just a ballplayer. I want to be a person.

"Back home I like for people to think of me more as a good hunter than as a baseball player," he said.

But it was becoming hard for them to do that. For several years now the sign on Route 13 leading into this town of 2,300 citizens has had a picture of Jim Hunter on it with the inscription, WELCOME TO HERTFORD, HOME OF JIM (CATFISH) HUNTER. NEXT RIGHT—GO FOUR BLOCKS.

Ask additional directions and a native will tell you, "You can't miss it. His driveway is as wide as the interstate. And he's got the biggest and the smartest and the most hunting dogs around."

Many of the Ahoskie townspeople did not like the notoriety the Catfish case brought their town. Ramona Stott, a secretary with the town newspaper, said, "Folks were interested, or shall I say, 'ticked off,' at TV news stations callin' Ahoskie the sticks. What we were payin' attention to were all the slams and innuendos."

Reporter Jeanette Davis added, "All the reporters who

came to town acted real sweet. It was, 'Please this,' and 'Thank you,' and, 'Isn't this a swell little country town.' Then they'd walk outta here and write trash. Or they'd get on TV and say, 'And this is Joe Blow, signing off from the boonies.'"

Sports editor Chris Powell said, "It's pretty clear their theme was, 'Country boys pull a fast one on the city slickers.' They showed TV shots that made it look like Ahoskie is one of the all-time hick towns."

The youngster added, "I think everyone was interested in what happened with Hunter, but not personally involved. The town got more behind the Ahoskie Cougars, who went on to the state football championship. I mean they could sit in the stands there, but not in the law office."

The young AP rep, Ricky May, said, "Baseball here is nothing, this is football country."

The nearby Washington Redskins long have been this state's "home team" in pro footfall and send their telecasts here. Sonny Jurgensen and Roman Gabriel both came out of Wilmington, North Carolina. Sonny played at Duke; Gabriel at North Carolina State. Ken Willard played at the University of North Carolina.

All three schools have been outstanding in basketball, of course. David Thompson led North Caroina State to an undefeated season in 1973 and the NCAA title in 1974.

The Carolina Cougars of the American Basketball Association, which played in Charlotte, Greensboro, and Raleigh before becoming "The Spirits of St. Louis," and the Charlotte Hornets of the World Football League, who inherited the New York Stars at midseason of the rebel league's first season, have been the state's only "major league" professional sports representatives.

What this really is, more than anything else, is stock car racing country. The Pettys, father and son, Lee and Richard, three-time and six-time NASCAR Grand National champions, hail from the Randleman-High Point area, and are the true heroes of fans in this state. The Super Speed-

James Roark, Los Angeles *Herald-Examiner*

The Catfish in action.

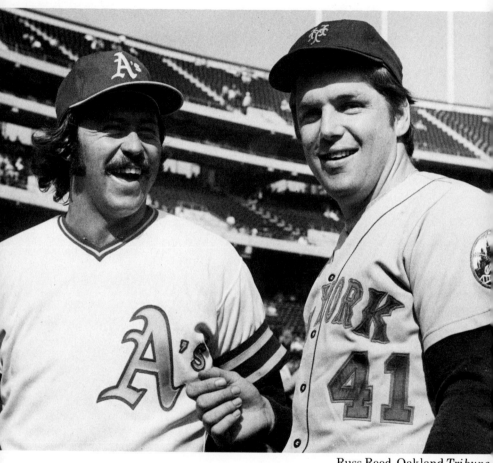

Before he made it to New York, the Catfish chats with the Big
Town's other superstar pitcher, Tom Seaver of the Mets.

ways at Charlotte and Rockingham host two major races each every year, which jam these arenas.

But baseball interest always has been big in North Carolina, and since Oakland's run on World Series championships, ol' Catfish Hunter has surpassed the pitching Perrys, Gaylord and Jim, as the Tar Heel pride and joy. Whenever the A's were playing along the Eastern Seaboard, transistor radios throughout the state were tuned in.

The auction of the A's star brought headlines in the *Herald,* which read, AHOSKIE A HOUSEHOLD WORD NOW. And reporter Davis said of teen-age sports editor Powell, "Chris'll never be the same. A coupla teams sent him their official caps and it made him very happy. He thinks this was the greatest thing to happen to Ahoskie and second only to us gettin' a major league team."

Allowing as to how Ahoskie was not exactly in line for a big league franchise, Chris Powell did say, "Yup, everyone was excited about bein' on the national scene."

An editorial in the newspaper worried about their community being given a hick-town image and decided the outside world was jealous:

"We suspect Americans long for the virtues symbolized by country lawyers and hick towns. It's places like Ahoskie that are the envy of millions who live in the major metropolitan areas. . . ."

It wasn't all bad, after all, the *Herald* concluded:

"If we play it right, one day we'll erect a statue to Charles Finley, who made it all possible."

Many of the natives were most concerned that Hunter's head not be turned by the money thrown at him and that he remain the country boy they'd known.

Sports editor Powell said, "Jim's down to earth. He's the same person he's always been. He may be a star, but he doesn't act like one."

Added lawyer Carlton Cherry: "He has a sense of values. He's as good a family man as anybody I've ever seen."

Mrs. Craig Vaughn of the Tomahawk Motel said, "I've known Jimmy since he was sixteen and pitching for our Legion team. I know his brother Pete even better because he taught my daughter in the eighth grade of our local school, but I know Jim, too.

"He's a fine boy, real wholesome and plain living. Just an all-around boy. We're all proud of him. We think he deserves the money, and I know it won't go to his head."

"Money spoil Jim Hunter? No way!" said Curt Blefray, the former teammate whose letter may have helped land Catfish for the Yankees. "Nothing can spoil Jimmy. He's a super guy. He's just people. He's the Number One guy, which is why I wrote him a letter telling him to sign with the Yankees, the Number One organization in baseball. That's why I'm glad he stuck it to Finley. Jimmy's the kind of guy you want for a friend, not for an enemy."

Reggie Jackson, now also an ex-teammate, added, "Everyone on the A's considered him their friend. There were other guys on the team I felt closer to, but everyone felt close to him. He's a very simple human being, very decent. He's a dynamite guy, a lot of fun, and you have fun being with him. You don't have to put yourself out to get to know him.

"He's a stand-up guy. That's why none of the guys on the team that I talked to resented his leaving. We'll miss him, but we'd all do the same thing if we had the chance. He didn't try to hide his intentions and he didn't sneak away. He was well-liked and he still is.

"I always felt with Catfish that if I ever lied to him, he'd never forgive me. He's the kind of guy who if he gives you his word, that's it. And he expects the same thing in return. He was loyal to Finley and the A's until he stopped getting loyalty in return.

"Money won't change him. He was shortchanged for years, but money never meant a lot to him. It's kind of funny that he should be the one to fall into a pile of it. He'll take it, but he'll give you value in return. He's a money player.

"He can play the whole game. And when the chips are piled high on the table, he's the guy you want dealing. He's tough. He can be mean. Pressure doesn't bend him. He's a pro. He just goes out there and does the job, turn after turn, season after season. And he does his job better than anyone in baseball.

"He doesn't have the best fastball or the best curveball or the best change-up, but he's the best pitcher in baseball. He's the best pitcher in baseball because he's the most consistent winner and because he does the most when it means the most. Whether you pay him a dime or a dollar, he'll get the job done any way it has to be done.

"He's not charismatic, except in the record books. He looks plain and simple out there. You think you can hit him, but you can't. Not when it counts. Not often. He's human. But he's less human than the next guy. On the field. Off the field, he's a real human being. On the field, he's inhuman."

14

During the baseball season Catfish Hunter lives like a baseball player. He looks like they look these days. Since Charlie Finley's promotional "Mustache Day" in 1973, when he paid his players to grow mustaches, many of them have kept their mustaches and he has a big one. He has let his hair grow long, the way athletes wear their hair nowadays. He dresses in Edwardian sports coats, ruffled shirts, and bright, bell-bottomed trousers. He drives a fancy car.

As writer Ron Bergman of the Oakland *Tribune* points out, Hunter knows big cities now, and he acts as if he has been around: "He knows how to hail a cab, read a menu, and order a drink. He has a machismo sense of humor that wouldn't endear him to Gloria Steinem's social circles, but serves to make him a man's man among his teammates, who all regard him with an appreciative affection."

He himself, however, admits, "I'll never be at home in big cities." Before he dealt himself to New York, he confessed, "New York still scares me to death. And I act like a hick from the sticks when I get to L.A. I used to visit Disneyland every trip in until the guys started to make fun of me for it. I've learned how to live the life you live in big league baseball, but a lot of it don't come natural to me."

He never has sought the spotlight and never has liked being interviewed and talking about himself. Until he won the Cy Young Award and the big baseball auction in 1974, he was one of the least-publicized superstars in sports. He says this was because he "never was good to reporters."

Actually, he almost always has cooperated with the

press, but he seldom has had much to say. "I just don't believe in popping off," he says. "I believe if you can't say anything nice about someone, it's better not to say anything at all. I don't knock my owner, my managers, my teammates, or my opponents. I know I'm not good copy.

"And I don't act colorfully off the field. I don't put myself in positions where I could get bad publicity. I'm not a goody-goody, but I am sort of straight. I'm a family man at heart and I don't run around."

Although the A's always were fighting with one another, no one ever fought with the Catfish. "I don't believe fistfights prove anything," he says.

While Blue Moon Odom was fighting Vida Blue, and Reggie Jackson was fighting Mike Epstein, and Billy North was fighting Reggie Jackson, and Rollie Fingers was fighting Blue Moon Odom, and Blue Moon Odom was fighting Reggie Jackson, Catfish Hunter was staying strictly out of it.

Yet, Hunter has a bit of the devil in him. In 1974, the star relief-pitcher for manager Alvin Dark's A's, Rollie Fingers, was having problems holding his marriage together. It was the Catfish who clipped a cartoon from a newspaper and taped it to Rollie's locker. It showed a man and woman in bed together, with the woman saying to the man, "I told Alvin we were washed up, but I said it soft in case I want to make up with him."

All of the A's thought it was funny except Fingers. When he saw it, he tore it down and demanded to know who had put it up. When no one was willing to admit to it, Fingers demanded that his teammates quit talking about his personal problems. They did so until before the first World Series game, when Odom made a wisecrack that sent Fingers flying at him.

From the dugout, Hunter rides foes frequently and sometimes nastily. He is considered a rough bench jockey. And when the A's pitchers were down on Dark for removing them from games too fast too often, Hunter would sometimes sit in the bullpen between starts and holler at Alvin, "Attaway, Alvin. Nice move, Alvin. That's thinking in there, Alvin."

At one point during the season, Dark deprived Hunter of a shutout simply because he wanted to give another pitcher some work in the ninth inning of a one-sided game. At season's end, Hunter lost the shutout title of the American League to Luis Tiant by the margin of one. Yet at season's end, when Hunter beat Baltimore in the game that gave the A's their third straight pennant, he said he dedicated the victory to Dark, "who has had to handle so much heat and has stood up to it so well."

Hunter has been among the most thoughtful of the A's, often remembering teammates' birthdays and anniversaries and always welcoming them and their families into his home. When John Donaldson, an obscure minor-league-level player, was permitted to sit on the A's bench for the final month of the 1974 season so he could complete four years' service in the majors and thus qualify for a pension, Hunter was the only player who made note of it. On behalf of himself, his wife, Helen, and their two children he sent Donaldson a card—"From the four of us for your fourth."

He is thus, like most people, more complex inside than he may seem on the surface. If he is imperfect, who isn't? He has his strengths and his weaknesses. His strengths seem to outnumber his weaknesses by a good many. He has a temper, but controls it most of the time. Twice in moments of frustration he has been known to slam doors in newsmen's faces. But he treated the writers as if nothing had happened the next time they met. Most of the time, even in bad times, he would talk to the writers.

He usually speaks slowly, often staring at the ground, taking his time before answering questions, but he will answer; he just wants to make sure he says just what he wants to say.

He is a private person who does not like to give a lot of himself away to strangers.

He would prefer to do his job and let his performances speak for themselves.

Pitching coach Wes Stock says, "Catfish Hunter has become the best in baseball because he's never satisfied with himself; he's always trying to improve. When I was with Milwaukee in 1972, Catfish was slumping and he asked what he was doing wrong. He's not ashamed to ask advice of anyone, even someone on the other team. And a baseball man is not above giving help to a rival if he respects him. You have to respect Hunter.

"I gave him a couple of tips that might have helped him. But what was important was that he was willing to look for help, to try to do something different. He always wants to improve. He never takes his position for granted. So he keeps getting better and better. I don't think he's approached his peak yet. He may not win as much with a worse team than the A's, but he'll pitch as well.

"Other pitchers may be better from year to year, but over a stretch of a few years, nobody's been better."

A perfectionist about pitching, he is a stickler for details. "Those little things, they add up," he drawls.

For example, although he is not a night owl, he stays up late into the wee hours of the morning many nights, especially before he is due to pitch and sometimes after he has pitched. "The reason is," he says, "when I go to bed, I want to go to sleep, not lie there worrying. I want to be tired enough to fall asleep.

"I don't need a lot of sleep. I may go to bed at one thirty or two and get up at eight. That's enough sleep for anyone. I rest the day of a night game I'm going to pitch. I'm not much for running around, anyway. And I want to feel strong when I take the mound."

On the mound he is all business. Although he chews tobacco off the field, he chews gum on the field. "I like tobacco best, but in a game sometimes I swallow it and get sick, so I chew gum instead," he confesses, smiling.

When he broke into the majors in Kansas City, he even

buddied up to the ball-park groundskeeper there, George Toma, to learn as much as possible about how the playing field in general and the pitcher's mound in particular were prepared. "I was practically part of the ground crew," Catfish confesses. "Before game time I would go out to the mound and doctor up the pitching surface to my liking."

Toma learned how Hunter liked it. Since the team transferred to Oakland and returned to oppose the new team in Kansas City, the groundskeeper has been keeping conditions just the opposite from the way Catfish wants them.

Hunter laughs and says, "Now George tells me, 'You don't pitch for us anymore; you're the enemy.' Now, hell, every time I go out there to pitch he has two inches of mud on the mound. Between the mud on the mound and the rock-hard infield and the Astroturf outfield a pitcher like me who makes the batters hit the ball doesn't have a chance.

"The guy is a genius with a rake and hose. I can't fault him for doing his job. His work is to handle the grounds and to do whatever he can within legal limits to help the Royals win. My job is to help my team win. But because of him I have won less here than anywhere else."

Toma says, "He relies a great deal on the shape and condition of the mound. In his early years he gave me some of the credit for his wins. I did my best to help him when he was here. Now I do my best to hinder him. The team can use the help. He's not easy to beat."

Hunter has an easy motion. Concealing the ball behind his glove, he raises his left knee waist-high as he rocks back, swings the leg forward as he takes a long stride, and throws three-quarters overhand with his right hand. His motion alters little from pitch to pitch. He does not wear himself out.

Depending on the preferences of his various managers, Hunter has been ready to pitch every fourth or fifth day in turn with few exceptions throughout his career. Former teammate Paul Lindblad, a pitcher, says, "I never saw him fake it once in all the years I've watched him. I've heard guys say, 'Hell, I'm not going out there.' Not him. I've seen him pitch with injuries. Every fourth or fifth day you hand him the ball and he's ready to throw it."

His first two seasons in the majors, Hunter started 20 and 25 games. The following eight years he started 34 to 41 times every year and pitched from 230 to 318 innings every year.

He throws a fastball, a slider, and a change-up. His fastball is not overpowering and has no hop to it, but it moves around. His slider is a small curve. His change-up offers just enough variety from his fastball to keep the batters off balance.

He keeps the batters off balance. What he throws, he throws where he wants. He has uncanny control of his pitches. If he just wanted to throw the ball over the plate, he'd never walk a batter. But he throws to batters' weaknesses and in the gray areas between strikes and balls.

He knows batters' weaknesses. He is a smart pitcher who studies batters and knows what they like to hit and what they find hard to hit, and he mixes up his pitches so they can't anticipate what they're apt to see.

Except in certain circumstances when men are on base and a strikeout is needed, he does not try for strikeouts. He tries to get the batters to hit the pitches he wants them to hit, pitches they will not hit well.

It is said that when Hunter pitches, fielders field. Unlike most pitchers, he is not afraid to pitch high. In fact, he prefers it. So the batters hit a lot of fly balls. One game, his first baseman did not make a single putout. But Hunter won the game.

Wes Stock says, "You'd be surprised at the number of pitchers in the majors who are afraid to throw strikes because they figure the hitter can hit strikes. They try to get him to hit bad balls and wind up walking a lot and getting in trouble. They lack confidence in their control and so they won't cut corners and can't set batters up to hit the pitch they want the hitter to hit.

"Hunter's not scared to throw strikes and he's not afraid

of any hitter. He can cut the corners and set the batters up so they've got to swing at what he gives them. He wouldn't be afraid to throw strikes to Johnny Bench with the bases loaded. He wouldn't be afraid to throw strikes to anyone because there are strikes and there are strikes and Hunter's strikes are not fat pitches the hitter is expecting."

A's slugger Sal Bando says, "Hitters aren't afraid of Hunter. They know he's going to throw them pitches they can hit. But they don't hit them as well as they think they will. He fools you. He's one of the few who can dominate you with control.

"He's frustrating because he's harder to hit hard than you think he should be. And as the game goes on, he gets even harder to hit hard. A hitter that's been around and watched him work awhile, I guarantee you he's not that anxious to face Hunter in the seventh, eighth, or ninth innings."

Rival Brooks Robinson of the Orioles says, "You know he won't walk you, so you know you're going to have to get a hit off him to get on. You think you can hit him, but it's not as easy as it looks. You don't mind batting against him because you're not afraid he's going to hit you with a fastball and you know he's not going to blow you out of there and embarrass you, but he frustrates you when you get more hits than runs off him."

He hates to waste even one pitch. Thus, he seldom throws at hitters. He keeps them loose by putting the pitch where they least expect it to be, and by changing speeds on it all the time so they cannot time it properly.

A few years ago when the California Angels were trying to keep the Catfish from his twentieth victory of the season, he gave up one homer in the first inning and two more on consecutive pitches in the fourth inning. The third pitch of the fourth inning sent batter Billy Parker sprawling and Hunter didn't allow a run the rest of the way and won the game.

"I guess I got a little ticked off," Hunter drawled after the game. He confessed it was not his style to try to intimidate batters and to blow his cool. But he hinted that if that was what he had to do that game to win that game that was what he would do. One home run was all right. Maybe even two. But three! The Cat got tough and turned things around.

Normally, he'll let the hitters hit—as long as they hit to the fielders.

"I figure if we can get some runs and make the plays in the field, we can win when I pitch. I figure it's a team game and I expect my fielders to participate in my pitching," Catfish comments. "The way I figure it, I can pitch a lot more regularly and a lot longer if I don't try to overpower the opposition."

Former A's catcher Dave Duncan says, "He's the perfect pitcher for a catcher. He goes over the batters with you and you know how he wants to work on the hitters. He's very easygoing. If you disagree, he'll go with your call as fast as he will his own. If you call curveball and he's thinking fastball, he just reprograms himself for your pitch. This makes him an easy man to catch."

Another who caught Hunter with the A's, Ray Fosse, says, "He's the easiest pitcher I've ever had to catch. He doesn't throw as hard as some and his ball doesn't move around as much as some and when he's supposed to pitch a certain place, he'll put it in that place. He won't shake you off more than three or four times a season. When he does, it's more of a matter of where he wants to pitch than it is what. He figures he can make any pitch work if he puts it where he wants it."

A's catcher-first baseman Gene Tenace says, "He's the best pitcher I've ever seen to play with because he always does what he's supposed to do. The fielders can play him certain places because they know he'll put his pitch in the place it's supposed to be and the batter is apt to hit it to certain places.

"There is no question that he has benefited from the sort of support the A's give a pitcher. We may not hit for average, but we hit when hits mean runs. We may not score a lot of runs, but we score as many as we need to win. We know how to win. People overlook that we make the plays in the field. They don't show up in the box score, but a hit you take away from another team is as good as one you get. Guys like Dick Green have won for us even with .200 batting averages because they make the plays that have to be made in the field. And the thing with Hunter is he uses his fielders; he lets them do what they do best."

Third baseman Sal Bando says, "He's so easy to play behind. He doesn't take a lot of time out there. You're on your toes all the time because you know he's working fast and you know the ball's going to be hit somewhere. Once in a while, the ball will be hit hard, but most of the time the batters only get a little piece of it and you can make a play on it."

Left fielder Joe Rudi says, "Most of the balls hit off him are hit up in the air, but not many are hit hard. He'll give up home runs, but he'll also give a lot of soft fly balls. He keeps the outfielders busy, but you know what to expect from him and he doesn't disappoint you. When we learned how to execute the plays you must make to win, we started to win. The Cat executes."

Until the designated hitter arrived in the American League, Hunter used to help himself with his hitting. He's a good hitter. Former teammate Mike Epstein says, "He may have been the best-hitting pitcher in baseball." His won-and-lost record benefited because he seldom was pinch-hit out of close games.

Also, he's always helped himself with his fielding. He's a fine fielder. Epstein says, "He executes perfectly all the plays a pitcher has to make in the field. He's quick on bunts. He hustles to first. He knows when to throw to the first baseman and when to take the throw from him. He backs up plays. He's an all-around athlete."

Hunter doesn't beat himself.

Hunter has not struck out as many as 200 foes in a season, but he also never has walked as many as 100. He struck out only 143 foes in 1974, 224 fewer than did Nolan Ryan, but Hunter walked only 46, 156 fewer than Ryan, and Hunter won three more games and lost four fewer games.

Ryan also pitches no-hitters. Although Hunter pitched his perfect game in his fourth season in the majors, he was only learning how to pitch at that time, it is not the sort of pitching he has developed, it just was one of those games when everything worked for him and it really is not his style.

On his best days Ryan is better than Hunter. On his best days, Ryan is better than anyone. But Hunter has more good days than Ryan. Most days Hunter is better. Ryan can be overpowering, but Hunter is craftier, works easier, and so is more consistent.

Hunter does not give up many home runs when the game hangs in the balance. He'll give up hits in the early parts of games or when his team is far ahead, but not often in tight spots. He seems to pitch only as hard as he has to in order to win. If he needs a shutout to win, he is capable of it.

However, he is clearly unconcerned about earned-run averages and such statistics.

"If you make 'em hit—and I'm the kind of pitcher who makes the hitters hit—you're gonna get hit hard once in a while," he admits. "But if I've got a run to spare, I don't mind giving up a run. I'd rather have a man hit a home run off me with one swing of the bat than have a team score a run on me with three hits. I don't embarrass easy and I don't want to work any harder than I have to.

"Now, when I don't have a run to spare, I'm as careful as I can be. I don't mind giving up runs, but I don't want to give up so many we don't have one more run than they do in the end. I don't care how I win, just so I win. It don't have to be pretty."

Reggie Jackson says, "If the Cat has a big lead in the eighth he'll just lay it in there and make them hit it. He doesn't care if he beats you eleven to ten as long as he beats you. Some guys can't win eleven to ten. It isn't in them. If they give up a few runs, they give up. If they give up a few runs in the first inning, they think the game's over.

"The Cat never gives up. If he gets off to a bad start, he just bears down harder. I've seen him give up six runs in the first inning and then hang on to win, seven to six. Getting roughed up doesn't bother Catfish; he just comes right back at you. He's a competitor. He's as hard to beat on bad days as on good days.

"That's the mark of a real competitor. The Cat's a competitor."

Pat Jordan wrote in *Sports Illustrated,* "Hunter is the kind of pitcher who wears down the opposition in the same relentless way that the sea wears away a piece of land. The process is invisible, only the result is apparent."

Former A's manager Dick Williams says, "Hunter is a grinder. He just keeps going out and grinding you down and grinding out victories." The A's current manager, Alvin Dark, says, "He doesn't look as good as his record. Everyone thinks he's easy to hit, but after a while they realize he's hard to beat."

Williams says, "He's a modern Robin Roberts. Everyone always got a lot of hits and runs off Robin, but they didn't get a lot of wins off him." Dark says, "He's a lot like Ed Lopat. He doesn't have a lot of stuff, but he knows how to use what he has and he wins with it. He makes the most of himself, which few athletes do."

Roberts says, "He does remind me a lot of myself. I won two hundred eighty-six games in nineteen years and I guess I never looked good getting them. He won one hundred sixty-one games in his first ten years and maybe he hasn't looked much better, but he's on a similar pace. I still hold the major league mark for giving up forty-six home runs in a season. But I won nineteen games that year. Most years at that time I won twenty or more. They hit homers off Hunter, too, but he wins."

Lopat says, "Catfish can throw harder than I could, but he doesn't depend on speed. I threw a lot of what they called junk. He throws fewer pitches. But we both put what we throw where we wanted. I was a control pitcher and so is he. There's a lot of ways to beat the batters. You can overpower them or you can outsmart them. Catfish is like I was; he outsmarts them.

"Coming to New York it's only natural to compare Catfish to Tom Seaver, who is now the other top pitcher in town. But you can't compare them because they're different types of pitchers. Seaver tries to overpower you, Catfish tries to outsmart you. Seaver is super. He's won twenty or more three times. But one year he wins twenty, the next year he doesn't. Catfish wins twenty every year, four straight years coming into New York."

For his first five seasons Hunter struggled along as less than a .500 pitcher as he mastered his trade. His records were 8–8, 9–11, 13–17, 13–13, and 12–15. By his sixth season he was learning how to pitch and he put together an 18–14 mark. Since then he has strung seasons of 21–11, 21–7, 21–5, and 25–12.

The 25-victory season stands out, of course, but his performance was equally outstanding the season before. Few remember that he was struck on the pitching hand by a batted ball in the All-Star Game and missed almost a month of starts, or else he probably would have won at least 25 games that season and have put two 25-victory campaigns back to back.

His earned-run average frequently has been above three a game and seldom has been among baseball's best in a given season. In his 21–5 season it was 3.34, which is considered poor. But in his 21–7 season it was at 2.04, which is superb. Since the wins and losses were comparable, it is clear the ERA's were deceptive.

In his 25–12 season of 1974, he led the league with a 2.49 ERA average. Still, he wasn't satisfied with his season. "I lost too many games," he says simply. "I won two out of three decisions, which was all right, but I lost too many. You get twenty-game winners who are also twenty-game losers. What's the point? How do they help their teams?

"The only statistic I care about is winning percentage. I like those wins, but they have to go with a good winning percentage to mean much. If you've won ten or fifteen more games than you've lost, then you've done your job, then you've helped your team."

For four straight seasons, Hunter had won at least 10 more games than he'd lost. For his 10 years in the majors he had won 58 percent of his decisions and for the last four years he'd won 71 percent of his decisions.

"His greatest asset is consistency," comments Mike Hegan, a former teammate. "He's not going to impress you in one game, but over a season you realize he's some kind of pitcher. And when it does come down to one game, he's an even better pitcher."

"I can sum him up in one word," says another former teammate, Paul Lindblad. "Cool. He never gets hot and bothered. He never gets excited. He's so calm, he calms you down. He's so confident, he gives you confidence. Most of the pressure has been on him in pressure games but he produces under pressure. When he'd pitch, we'd feel the pressure wasn't so heavy."

Dick Williams says, "The A's have been fortunate to have two pressure pitchers like Catfish Hunter and Ken Holtzman. Holtzman has responded to World Series pressure about as well as has Hunter. And relievers like Rollie Fingers and Darold Knowles have held up superbly under pressure. But I think Hunter set the style for his teammates."

Alvin Dark says, "If I had to pick one pitcher to pitch one game, then I'd pick Catfish. I think all the A's felt that way."

Rival manager Sparky Anderson of the Reds, hurt by Hunter in a World Series, says, "There hasn't been a better pressure pitcher than Hunter in recent years and few better in all the years I've been around."

Another rival manager, Walter Alston of the Dodgers, also hurt by Hunter in a World Series, concedes, "Catfish comes through in the clutch. You know you're going to have to go out and scratch for anything you get off him in a big game. You know he won't give you anything."

Reggie Jackson says, "The few times he's been beaten in pennant games or play-off games or World Series games it came as a shock to us. We just couldn't believe it. Come to think of it, I don't believe he ever has been beat in a World Series game. When he lost a play-off game, it shook us up. But then we pulled ourselves together because we knew he wouldn't lose another one.

"You know, when ballplayers or managers get together and they talk about who's the best pitcher, there's this pitcher or that pitcher they talk about, there's a lot of good pitchers, but when they get to talking about pressure pitchers in big games, there's only one pitcher left and that's the Cat and you forget all the rest.

"To a baseball man, coming through in the clutch is what counts, and the Cat comes through in the clutch. I don't care who you're talking about—Seaver, Palmer, even Koufax. Hell, even Cy Young and Walter Johnson. You can dig 'em out of the grave. Ain't none of 'em going to do better because there's no way to do more than win. Can't anyone have been better than Hunter in a big game."

A's captain Sal Bando says, "It's just guts. Hunter's not afraid of anyone or anything. Most money pitchers, they're not afraid to challenge the big hitters. There just aren't that many money pitchers around. There's a lot of good pitchers, but not many who get better the bigger the game is. And Hunter's the best. He's not afraid to challenge the best hitters and the best teams. He responds positively to a challenge.

"It's easier to be a money hitter than a money pitcher. I'm considered a money hitter, so I know. A hitter has four chances or more to get a big hit in a big game. A pitcher has only one chance. He has to work inning after inning, but he can get beat in any inning, on any pitch. He can never relax. And if he makes a mistake he may not get a chance to make up for it the way a hitter can."

"It's character, plain and simple," says Alvin Dark. "Catfish has character. On and off the field. The kind of person he is off the field reflects in the way he performs on the field. He always gives you all he has and he has a lot to give. And in a big game he digs down deep and comes up with that little bit extra that makes the difference. He's a winner the way few players are."

Twice Hunter has won the games that produced pennants for the A's. He won three times in five play-off decisions for them and one of the losses was in his first play-off. He's won four times in four World Series decisions. His lifetime earned-run average entering the 1975 season was above three per game. But three times his earned-run average in play-offs or World Series was under two a game. One play-off it was 1.17 and one World Series, the 1974 classic, it was 1.17.

He seldom relieves, but when he was asked to pitch relief in the 1974 World Series he came through in the clutch. He seldom strikes out foes, but when he needed a strikeout he got one. He was brought into the ninth inning of the first game with two out, one man on base, and a one-run lead. He struck out Joe Ferguson to end the game.

"He didn't show me anything," Ferguson griped later. Hunter seldom shows anyone anything. He just wins.

"I don't care how I win, just so I win," Catfish admits. "I have a sign in my locker that says, 'Winning isn't the only thing, but wanting to is.' I believe that. I can live with losing as long as I know I did everything I could to win. What ticks me off is when I've lost my concentration and not worked the way I should've.

"There are times, especially against weaker teams or at times when the game doesn't seem to mean as much, when I catch myself thinking about hunting or fishing or some such thing out there on the mound and that really makes me mad. There isn't any team so weak they can't beat you at any time if you don't beat them first. And every loss hurts. And when it's one you should have won it hurts even more.

"I haven't got an overpowering fastball like Vida Blue or Nolan Ryan and I can't break off a curveball the way Burt Blyleven can, but my fastball moves a lot and my slider breaks enough to keep the batters off stride and I've got a good change-up that keeps them even more off stride. I've been developing the change-up and now I can throw at several different speeds to throw off the hitters' timing.

"When you've got real good control of your fastball, it doesn't make any difference how fast you throw it. You hit the right spot, they're not going to get the real good wood on the ball. You don't always hit the right spot. I have real good control and I don't always. That's why they get the real good wood on the ball sometimes. Sometimes too often and you lose. But percentage-wise I'm going to put the ball where I want it most of the time most games and so I win most of the time. I can control all my pitches. I won't waste any.

"Maybe I do pitch better in the big games. Maybe I concentrate more. If you can pitch the ball good enough to win, concentration will determine whether you win or lose most games. You need support, but if your pitching keeps you in most games, you'll win your share. And the bigger the game is, the easier it is to concentrate because you don't have to psych yourself up, you know you have to be up to win. And maybe once you've won some of 'em, you stop being afraid of 'em.

"I know I'd rather pitch in 'em than watch 'em because I get too nervous sitting on the bench just looking. If I can get in there, I can do something about winning. I've won enough of 'em to have confidence I'll win and to give the guys behind me confidence we'll win. Confidence is a lot of the battle. I don't have a big ego, but I know I'm good. I'll leave it to others to decide just how good, but I know I can win. I expect to win. I don't expect to lose. When you lack confidence, you try to win, but you expect to lose.

"Heck, I've been there before, I've been through it and I've done it. I figure if I'm good enough to begin with and I want to win more than the other guy and I expect to win more than he does, I'll beat him. A big game, I know it's not just another game, but I try to pitch like it was. If I can, I'll be OK, because a big game, the other team isn't going to play their usual game. Not like I will. How can they? They haven't won and I have. Experience pays off. Especially experience winning.

"I used to watch Ed Lopat win when he won with experience. Experience and control was about all he had. He couldn't throw it hard enough to hit you 'side of the head to hurt you. He knew where he was throwing the ball. He had a good breaking ball and he could work it around. When you can throw two or three pitches over the plate for strikes, that's when you can win. He could and it didn't matter how fancy the pitches were."

Clyde Kluttz says, "Jimmy could always throw strikes, even as a youngster."

Jim Hunter says, "It's one of the first things I learned, and maybe the most important. I get a kick out of it when I'm compared to Eddie Lopat or Robin Roberts because they were the pitchers I liked the most and looked at the hardest and learned the most from when I was growing up.

"I don't know if I knew then that I didn't have an overpowering fastball, because it was fast enough for kids' games and high school and American Legion ball, but I always leaned to the smart pitcher and tried to copy what they did that won for them.

"I remember my father taking me to Philadelphia to see a game and we saw Robin Roberts and my dad said Roberts didn't pitch hard enough to get him out, and I remember saying Roberts didn't have to pitch hard, he pitched smart and he got everyone out. I think he could hum the ball, but he didn't depend on that, he pitched real easy and smart, and so he lasted a long time, and I admired that more than anything."

Jim Hunter sighs and says, "I didn't get to the top overnight. I started back as a boy and I struggled through a lot of difficult learning years when I first got to the majors and it took a long time. Baseball isn't hard work the way farming is, but it's not easy to become good at it and most of us who maybe aren't naturals have to put a lot into it if we're going to get out of it what there is for us in it."

15

When the Yankees landed Catfish Hunter, after acquiring Bobby Bonds, there was the feeling in New York that they had captured the pennant for the 1975 American League season. They had, after all, not lost the 1974 flag until the final day of that season and then finished only two games behind Baltimore.

The Yankees seemed solid. The 25-game winner, Hunter, had joined 19-game winners George "Doc" Medich and Pat Dobson to form the nucleus of an outstanding starting staff. "Sparky" Lyle, who had won or saved 24 games the year before, bulwarked a good bullpen.

Although Bobby Murcer had driven in around 90 runs a year for four years for the Yankees, his replacement, Bonds, was supposed to add speed and punch to a batting attack which had produced only one man who hit 20 home runs the year before.

The Yankees had a lot of players of potential, such as Chris Chambliss, Graig Nettles, Ron Blomberg, Elliott Maddox, Lou Piniella, and Roy White, who were expected to have big seasons. Thurmon Munson gave them one of the best catchers in baseball.

Some of these, however, seemed big only in the Big Town. There really was nothing in their histories to justify the feeling that they were ready to become big stars. As it turned out, some were destined to have better years than the year before, some worse seasons. Which is the way it usually is.

In 1975 Chambliss, Nettles, and Munson had their best years ever, but Medich, Dobson, and Lyle had bad years. Injuries all but destroyed the seasons for Maddox, Piniella, and Blomberg, and an injury held back Bonds most of the season as he became a one-legged ballplayer. Injuries may be bad luck, but they are part of baseball.

It doesn't matter how good a team looks on paper, it still has to win the games on the field.

Boston's Red Sox didn't look that good on paper going into the season, but two unheralded rookie sluggers, Fred Lynn and Jim Rice, gave them the boost they needed to become the best in the division. As usual, Baltimore's Orioles started slowly and finished fast, but they couldn't catch up.

The Yankees couldn't keep up. They started slowly, came with a rush to rise to the top late in June, but then fell back over the last three months to finish well back. Replacing manager Bill Virdon with the more exciting Billy Martin was worth more on paper than it was on the field. Martin did little better with the Yankees than Virdon had.

It was a team which lacked punch and power in support of its pitchers and got uneven performances from most of its pitchers. A couple of .200 hitters, Fred Stanley and Jim Mason, struggled at shortstop, a .250 hitter, Sandy Alomar, at second base. The defense was inconsistent and unexceptional. It was the sort of team which had the talent to win if it stayed healthy and put together top seasons, but that just didn't happen.

In the deep disappointment which surrounded the season, some considered Catfish a letdown. President Paul himself said in a summing up late in the year, Hunter had only a "fair year." Hunter's slow start may have contributed to this conclusion. However, if a few regarded him as overrated in the past, he was underrated in the present.

The fact is Hunter pitched as well as he had in other recent seasons, but suffered from lack of the sort of support he previously enjoyed. The Yankees simply were not the A's. As it turned out, the A's were not good enough to win without Hunter, and the Yankees were not good enough to win with him. But he was about as good as he had been.

Consistency is the Catfish's trademark and he was incredibly consistent while the Yankees were falling apart all around him. His may have been the most consistent pitching performance of modern times. He pitched 10 complete games in a row and 30 in all, the most since Bob Feller hurled that many full games back in 1946, surpassing all Yankee standards for this.

Hunter hurled 328 innings, his most ever in the majors. He required only 20 innings of relief all year, and only eight after his first three starts of the campaign, an incredible record of steadiness and durability. The bullpen crew could have gone on vacation when it was Catfish's turn to take the mound.

He won 23 games, second high for him only to the 25 he won the year before with stronger support. While he lost 14, many of those would have been won with more help. The Yankees scored three runs or less behind him no less than nine times. They were shut out when he worked three times. Twice in ten days he lost by 1–0. His earned-run average was a superb 2.50.

Catfish tossed seven shutouts, including two in a row. He won four games by one run, but lost five by one. He had a one-hitter, a two-hitter, and a three-hitter. He won six out of seven decisions two times and five out of six another time.

He won four out of four from his old team, the champion A's, in spotlighted, pressure-packed tests. He beat Baltimore the game that broke the Orioles on the day they dropped from the pennant race.

The awards go to the players who perform for the pennant winners. The awards didn't go to Catfish Hunter this season, but he personally pitched pennant-winning baseball and he may have been the best pitcher in baseball once again. He helped his team tremendously, even if it doesn't show in the standings.

The Yankees attracted more than 1,200,000 fans at home, the most since their last pennant-winning season, 1964. They drew more than 400,000 fans in the 19 starts he made at home. They averaged almost 23,000 fans each game he started at home. They averaged 3,600 more fans on the games he pitched than those he did not pitch. This translates into more than $300,000 in additional revenues, or more than enough to cover the cost of his salary.

"I had a good year, even if no one noticed," he said with a smile later. "It's never a satisfying season when your team doesn't win, but most seasons most teams don't win. I suppose I've been spoiled by the A's recent years. But there's always another year. The year had to come when the A's lose. The year will come when the Yankees win. I hope I can help."

He shrugged wistfully, and added, "It was a hard year. The spotlight was a little hot. I felt the heat. I don't think it affected my performance. I've been around. I knew enough to just go out and do the best I could. But I got a lot of attention I don't really like. I never knew there were so many questions a man could be asked to answer. And so many different ways to ask the same questions. It was a long, long season, that's for sure." He sighed.

It started with spring training in Fort Lauderdale and around Florida where the Yankees played their exhibition games. "Here comes the Goldfish," one of his new teammates greeted a grinning Hunter. Another noticed and commented on his suitcase, which was in the A's green and gold colors. "I guess I'll have to have the SOB repainted," Jim said with a laugh.

"How many innings do you want to work in the spring to get ready for the season?" manager Virdon asked.

"You're the manager," Hunter replied. "I just do as I'm told. I just want to be treated as one of the guys."

He spent most of the spring trying to blend into the scenery, but reporters cornered him wherever he went.

In his first start Dave Kingman of the Mets bombed him for two home runs. Hunter shrugged it off. "A couple of buddies came up from Carolina, and they'd never seen a home run," Catfish told the writers, "so I wanted to show them one or two."

He is not a spring pitcher. He does not blow the ball by

the batter. He spends the preseason period sharpening his control. He spends the early season period doing this, too. He is not an early-season pitcher. Still, he worked hard and well this spring.

Virdon concluded, "He does everything you have to do to win. He is totally dedicated to winning. He is everything I've heard him to be. If a team had twenty-five players like him it wouldn't need a manager. You don't need to manage him. You just give him the ball and let him pitch."

Hunter also spent a lot of the spring getting to know his new teammates. They found him a strong, straight individual who had not been altered by having fallen into a fortune.

Lou Piniella said, "It costs him more to feed his dogs than I make. But there's no jealousy toward him on this team. He can put money in all our pockets. We just wish we'd have had the opportunity to make it the way he has."

Rudy May said, "If you can't get along with Catfish, you can't get along with anyone."

Concluding the exhibition schedule with 14 victories and 17 defeats, Virdon said, "Exhibition games are meaningless. We're a better team than we've shown."

It was a while before they showed it, however, and as it turned out, they weren't much better.

The Yankees lost their opener in Cleveland as Medich was knocked out. And they lost their home opener to Detroit. Hunter went the distance but home runs by Willie Horton and Nate Colbert helped beat him, 5–3, before a disappointed Shea Stadium turnout of 26,212.

"They're not hitting any maiden when they hit a home run off of me. I threw twenty-six home-run balls last season and still won twenty-five games," Hunter said. "I was a little nervous out there. It was a big game in a way. But it was really just another game."

He looked at the crowd of reporters surrounding him as he sat, sweaty and weary, in the clubhouse. "In Oakland we had maybe two or three writers come around after games. Here we have twenty or thirty every game." He smiled. "I suppose I'll get used to it, but it's like a World Series every day around here, isn't it?"

The Yankees lost their first three before they won one. They lost 8 of their first 12. Hunter blew a 3–0 lead to lose his second start, getting knocked out in the eighth inning of a 5–3 loss to Boston. The Shea Stadium fans booed him on his way out. It was a bit early for that sort of thing, but Hunter shrugged later and said, "If I was in the stands I'd have booed me, too. I'm getting paid to win, and I'm not winning."

He lost his third start, too, in Detroit. Willie Horton hit a three-run home run off Hunter in the first inning and the Tigers batted Hunter out with another three-run burst in the fourth on their way to an 8–3 romp. Catfish kicked his glove through the dugout on his way to a shower.

He didn't lose his fourth start, but the Yankees did. He had a 7–3 lead when two hits knocked him out in the seventh inning. Lyle got the loss after the Red Sox rallied to win, 11–7, in Boston. Hunter sat for 20 minutes after the game trying to explain to the press that he couldn't explain it.

"I'm not worried," he said. "I'm not helping the team. I don't like it. But I don't intend to worry about it. I'm always a slow starter."

Almost everyone else was worried. But if the writers and broadcasters had done their homework they would have known that Hunter didn't win a game until the last days of April in either 1972 or 1973 and was only 10–8 as late as June, 1974, when he wound up 25–12.

The A's knew. Asked to comment, Ken Holtzman said, "If the Yankees are worried about Catfish, they're worried about the wrong man." Ray Fosse said, "He always comes on after the first few games." Reggie Jackson said, "Unless he dies, he'll still win his twenty. All he has to do to win that many is get up every morning and go out and pitch every fourth game. He's a superstar."

Hunter pitched like it in his fifth start, finally. In fact, he came within four outs of a no-hitter and held Milwaukee to three hits in a 10–1 victory before a cheering crowd of 41,493 fans on a Sunday afternoon in Shea Stadium.

A rookie named Sixto Lezcano stroked a single between short and third with two out in the eighth inning to spoil the no-hitter. Young Robin Yount homered with one out in the ninth to spoil the shutout.

"I think I've settled down now," a relieved, grinning Hunter said later.

One of his foes, a fellow by the name of Henry Aaron, whom Hunter had retired four times in a row, said, "He was all I expected him to be. He was a three-million-dollar pitcher."

The Yankees got a lift from it. They started to win and by the time Hunter came back to blank Baltimore, 5–0, on five hits, topping Oriole ace Jim Palmer, on the first of May, the Yankees had finally climbed to the .500 level at 10–10.

However, they fell back. They lost five in a row, three by 4–3 and one with Hunter in Baltimore by 3–1. They went into Oakland and lost their sixth in a row.

They called on Catfish as their "stopper" and he came through. Facing his old teammates, who admittedly were determined to defeat him, he was superb. He shut out the A's on two hits, 3–0.

He gave up a hit to Bill North in the third inning, but he was out stealing. The Cat gave up a single to Claudell Washington the next inning. That was it. He retired the last 18 A's in a row. He did not walk a man, threw only 23 called balls in a mere 88 pitches, and faced only 28 batters.

A's manager Alvin Dark admitted, "It was a masterpiece. He made us look bad. Well, he's done it for us, why shouldn't he do it to us?"

Sal Bando said, "I don't know what he was doing wrong earlier, but he was doing everything right this time. He puts that ball right where he wants it, right where you don't want it. He's uncanny. We wanted this one more than usual, but I guess he did, too."

Reggie Jackson said, "It was a matter of pride. We wanted to beat him even though we like him. He wanted to beat us even though he likes us. It was sort of a big game and in the big game the Cat is the best. He looks easy to beat, but he's the hardest to beat there is. His pitches look easy to hit, but you can't hit them. He has this sport down to a science. He's one of the few who can overpower you with control.

"It felt sort of funny, facing him, like I was going the wrong way in a tunnel. It was sort of like dreaming." Jackson sighed.

"It was a strange sensation," Catfish admitted after he was cheered off by the "enemy" crowd of 23,942 fans, each and every one furious at Finley for having let him get away. "I almost went into the A's dugout a couple of times. Sitting in my dugout, I caught myself rooting for them a few times. Old loyalties don't die easy. But when they were batting against me they were just guys with bats in their hands and I was all pitcher.

"It's extra-satisfying," he conceded.

However, after the Yankees lost the final game of the set the next night, their 11–17 record was the worst in the American League and the second worst in the majors. And when they were two-hit and shut out by Nolan Ryan in Anaheim the next outing, Medich losing, they fell even further.

Hunter went 10 innings to beat the Angels, 4–3, the next night. The Yankee returned home and lost two straight to the A's, before Hunter again beat his old teammates, 9–1, on four hits to the cheers of 53,248 fans in Shea. The A's were so frustrated, Jackson tried to bunt for the first time in three years, but failed to beat it out. "He'd struck me out my last two times up. I had to try something else," Reggie remarked later. "We'll beat him sooner or later . . . I think."

Virdon said, "The way he's pitching, no one can beat him. The last four starts he's pitched the best I've ever seen anyone pitch in all the years I've been in baseball." The fact was they were past mid-May and Hunter had won the only four games the Yankees had won the entire month.

"I didn't expect to stop the A's twice in a row the way I

(Compix, UPI)

did, but I've gotten into a good groove now and when I'm doing what I want to do—I'm winning," Hunter said.

Again, he hiked up his club and it went on a tear, winning six out of seven games, including an 11–7 conquest of Texas in which Hunter struggled and had to have help in the ninth. Then they took off on a 13-game road trip in which they won 10. Hunter was beaten in Kansas City, 3–0, but bounced back to blank Texas, 6–0, on one hit.

He had a no-hitter until Cesar Tovar singled with two out in the sixth inning. The only other Ranger to reach base was Toby Harrah, who was safe on an error in the third. Hunter did not walk a man as he awed a crowd of 38,714, second largest in the home team's history.

Jeff Burroughs, the previous season's American League MVP, said, "Hunter was heavy. He throws different pitches at different speeds over the corners of the plate and he destroys your balance and timing. He's an artist."

The Catfish commented, "Some games it seems easy, some games hard. You throw the same all the time, but the ball behaves differently from time to time. The thing is to hang in there and do your best and hope for the best no matter what happens."

He did just that his next out, hanging on to trim Minnesota, 7–4, despite two home runs and a single by hot-hitting Rod Carew. The Yankees reeled off eight victories in a row before Hunter bowed to the Angels, 5–3, to open a home stand the second week in June.

The Yankees split 12 starts on the stand. During this stretch, Hunter checked Chicago, 3–0, on four hits before a bat-day gathering of 53,562 fans in the big suburban saucer in New York.

Taking to the road, they swept four games in Detroit and three in Baltimore. The Catfish retired the first 17 batters to face him before settling for a 9–2 triumph in Detroit. He scattered four hits in winning, 3–1, in Baltimore.

The Yankees had surged to a 40–29 record and soared into first place in the American League East as they moved into Boston the last week in June for four critical contests near the midway mark in the campaign.

Boston won the opener, 6–1, behind Luis Tiant, bombing Dobson to the delight of 34,293 fans in little Fenway Park. A two-run triple by Fred Lynn and a home run by Carlton Fisk finished off the Yankees.

Boston won again the next night, 9–1, behind Rick Wise, ripping rookie Larry Gura as 35,392 fans hollered happily. Little Doug Griffin drove in four runs to finish off the Yankees for the second straight time.

The Yankees bounced back into the lead on Saturday afternoon by struggling to an 8–6 victory before another packed house. Munson drove home three runs and Dick Tidrow came out of the bullpen to bail out Medich.

But on Sunday afternoon, the Red Sox reclaimed the divisional lead as Roger Moret shaded Hunter and the Yankees, 3–2. Hunter held the Boston team to six hits, but wild or weak throws from the outfield helped the winners to two of their runs.

The Yankees never again this season led the league.

In fact, they swiftly fell far from the pace as they lost their next six starts and their losing streak stretched to seven before they beat Baltimore back at home. Hunter lost one to the Orioles before bouncing back to shut out Texas, 4–0.

At the All-Star Game break, the Yankees were only four games over the .500 level, five games behind Boston, and fading fast. Hunter surrendered two hits and three runs in the classic at Milwaukee and was charged with the 6–3 loss to the National League. The Catfish captured only one of his next three starts, but both defeats were by 1–0. He lost a five-hitter to Gaylord Perry and Texas. And he lost a three-hitter to Bill Lee and Boston. The latter was a bitter disappointment.

The late July series with the Red Sox represented the Yankees' last chance to vault back into contention. Virdon conceded, "I don't know if they can keep winning the way they have. I do know we have to start winning. And this is the place to start. I think we have to show them we can beat them."

In the first game of the four-game set, on Friday night before 40,165 spectators at Shea, the Yankees did, 8–6, routing Luis Tiant. Lou Piniella tripled in two runs in the third and singled in two more in the seventh as the Yankees shot to an 8–2 lead. The Red Sox rallied for four runs in the eighth, chasing starter Rudy May and reliever Lyle, before Tippy Martinez saved it.

But Boston bounced back the next afternoon in front of 37,387 disappointed New Yorkers, beating the Yankees, 4–2. Catcher Carlton Fisk drove in three of the Red Sox runs, including the decisive two. He doubled behind Lynn's triple to start the Red Sox scoring, then singled behind a double by Denny Doyle, a single by Carl Yastrzemski, and a walk to Lynn to sew it up.

The Sunday double-header, which drew 53,631 fans, proved decisive.

Catfish was called on to hurl the opener. He and Bill Lee were locked in a scoreless duel going into the ninth. Lynn was safe on an error by shortstop Mason and stole second as Hunter fanned Rice. Miller then slapped a two-out single to bring home an unearned run that settled the issue and dealt Hunter and the Yankees a bitter defeat.

The Yankees tried to turn it around in the last of the ninth, but Lynn made an incredible diving catch of a smash by Nettles to turn them aside.

Lee hurled a six-hit shutout and Roger Moret came back with another six-hit shutout in the nightcap as Rice ripped four hits, driving in two runs and scoring two to pace the visitors to a 6–0 triumph and a sweep of the twin bill. This shoved the Yankees back to the .500 level, shot the Red Sox to 60–40, created a 10-game gap, and left the New Yorkers out of the running.

Hunter sat sorrowfully in the gloomy dressing room later, sighed, and said, "I'm not used to losing the big ones. It hurts like hell. Well, it's another team, another year, and another game from the one I've been playing."

His old team, the A's, with talent aplenty to replace departed stars, were coasting toward another title in their division, the weakest of the four in the majors.

By the beginning of August the Yankees were struggling with key players sidelined by injuries, makeshift lineups, and the remaining regulars, run right out of hope, performing erratically. Virdon paid the price. He was replaced as manager by Billy Martin, who had just been replaced as manager of the Texas Rangers.

The Yankees took two from Detroit, then beat Cleveland in Virdon's last game as manager of the Yankees, so he left with a three-game winning streak. Hunter won the last one for him.

Martin had been a hustling little second-base star for the Yankees years before, traded from the team because he had been involved in brawls, had criticized management, and been rated a troublemaker.

Moving into the managerial ranks, the fiery, inspirational leader took over troubled teams in Minnesota, Detroit, and Texas, swiftly turned the first two into divisional pennant-winners and the third into a contender, but was fired fast from each job.

Arguing with his superiors, fistfighting not only with foes, but with his own players and front-office officials, Martin was reluctantly released by superiors who rapidly ran out of patience with him.

Minnesota's Calvin Griffith said, "You can't talk to him. He always has to have the last word. He's not a team man. The front office is part of the team. With Martin, an owner feels his team getting away from him."

Martin shrugged and said, "I'm a winner. They say they want to win, and I win for them. If that's not enough for them, I don't know what else I can do for them. I know how to win. I know only one way. My way. If they think they can win another way, fine."

Without him, they did not win. After he was ousted, Minnesota and Detroit swiftly returned to the ranks of the also-rans. Despite the depression observed there, Texas president Brad Corbett decided he, too, had to give the gate to the controversial Martin at midseason, 1975.

Said Corbett with a sigh, "I love him like a son and I love what he did for our team, but you can't live with him. Everything has to be done his way. If you question him, he's ready to punch you in the nose. He has no respect for anyone's opinions but his own. You can't conduct business in a businesslike way that way."

Said Martin, "My way works. It's the only way I know to work. I know I have a temper. It's my greatest strength and my greatest weakness. I go all-out on and off the field. It's an asset on the field and a liability off the field.

"I suspect," he concluded, "I've had my last chance."

He guessed wrong. The Yankee season was lost. Desperate to generate new interest in the team and hold onto attendance the rest of the season, while stimulating new hope for the new season to come next year, Gabe Paul contacted Martin and offered to restore him to Yankee pinstripes.

Less than two weeks after he had been fired in Texas, Martin was hired in New York. President Paul admitted, "If Martin had not become available, Virdon would still be our manager. I have no complaints about the job Virdon did as our manager, but I have a greater enthusiasm for the job Martin may do."

So the managerial merry-go-round spun and spun. Soon it would spin Virdon into the skipper's seat in Houston as another field leader was fired. "This is the way it is with managers and coaches," Virdon observed. "You lose one job and win another. We become Gypsies, bouncing from team to team. It's senseless, but it's sports.

"Anyone who would manage or coach has to be a little crazy, but it gets in your blood," he said with a laugh.

Martin said, "I'm surprised but pleased at the way things turned out. Every time I get fired they say it's my last chance. This time I said it, too. But now I've got another chance and I mean to make the most of it. I've always felt like the Yankees were my team and now I feel like I've come home. I feel like this is a team that can win now. It can still win this season and it can win next season."

Had he changed? "Change? I can't change," he admitted, a smile spreading beneath his bushy mustache. "But the situation has changed. I've been assured I'll have a say on the players that will be respected. I have to learn I can't always have the last word. I'll listen to my bosses, if they'll listen to me.

"It's safe to say," he said with a laugh, "that I'll stir some things up."

The press and public were enthusiastic about Martin's return to New York. They could not care less about the friction he created behind closed doors. That was Paul's problem, which the team president had taken onto himself. All others cared about was that Billy the Kid was colorful and his clubs succeeded.

And the Yankees did win their first two starts under his stewardship to stretch their winning streak to five straight before bowing. In fact they won six out of his first eight starts and seemed about to surge back into contention before they blew three straight to the lowly Angels in Anaheim the second week in August.

Thus, ironically, it was Dick Williams, the original choice to become Yankee manager before Virdon, who presided over the death blow dealt the New Yorkers.

The former championship-winning manager of the A's had worked little improvement in his first full season as skipper of the Angels and they were bound for the bottom of the heap again, but they paused to pound the final nails in the Yankee coffin.

In Oakland, Finley laughed as though the gods had vindicated him. "When I look where Williams is with the Angels and where Hunter is with the Yankees, and where the A's are without them, I feel like I am having a last laugh. Williams didn't win for the A's. Hunter didn't win for the A's. If anyone won for them, I won for them. They are a team, they win as a team, and the team is bigger than its individuals. No man is indispensable here. Except maybe me." Charlie O chuckled.

As the Yankees struggled inconsistently through the last two months of the campaign, however, Jim Hunter was consistently successful. He pitched as he always pitched down the stretch, only this season he was on a club which was not contending for the pennant.

The Catfish captured his fifteenth victory of the season in Milwaukee the first Tuesday night in August with the help of a home run by Bonds in the ninth inning. In Oakland he made it three straight over the A's with a three-hitter, 3–1.

"There are times when I lose my concentration on the mound, when I start to think about home and hunting. Hell, you can't think about baseball all the time," he confessed. "But against my old teammates, I find I'm intense all the way. I guess I want to beat them more than other teams. It's a point of personal pride, I suppose."

He beat them again the last Tuesday night in August, at home, 7–1. This concluded his seasonal efforts against the A's at four for four and he had held the three-time champions to three runs in the four games. Billy Martin said, "Hunter is better than I thought he was. If I had four like him I'd be making plans for the World Series."

Reggie Jackson said, "He wants to beat us not only because we were his team, but because we've been the best team. He's the best pitcher and he wants to beat the best. He knows us better than he knows anyone else and so he can do what he does best better to us than to anyone else. He makes us look like Little Leaguers.

"We may get to the World Series without him, but it will be hard to win it without him," Jackson concluded.

"If they're in the World Series again, I'll be watching them and rooting for them," Catfish confessed. "But in front of a television set back home in North Carolina."

Finley was still saying he would have Hunter back on his roster by the World Series. His attorney, Neil Papiano, carried an appeal against the original ruling to an appellate court in San Francisco, contending he had a letter from Internal Revenue Service officials supporting the claim that the deferred payment provision in the original contract was illegal.

The court ruled against him, but Charlie O instructed his lawyers to carry the case further, to other courts to which they could still appeal. "I will not rest until I am vindicated," said the frustrated Finley.

Hunter shrugged. "I don't know anything about it and I don't want to hear anything about it. As far as I know I'm a Yankee for the rest of my career."

In his first start in September he hurled his sixth shutout of the season, stifling the Tigers in Detroit, 8–0, on six hits. He went the distance for the twenty-sixth time, tops in the majors and the most for a Yankee pitcher since Carl Mays in 1920.

In his next start Catfish captured his twentieth victory and seventh shutout, blanking Baltimore and beating Jim Palmer, 2–0, on six hits. The only previous American League pitchers to have won 20 games or more five straight seasons were Hall of Famers Walter Johnson and Lefty Grove.

"I've wanted to get up there with the greats all my life. I only hope I can stay there," Catfish commented. "I'm proud of the accomplishment. It stands for something special. It's a mark of consistency, which is the most important asset of a successful athlete.

"But I couldn't have done it without the support of my teammates. I'm not being modest. The Yankees have not been as successful as the A's have been in recent seasons, but I needed the backing they gave me just as much. You can't win alone."

Far from alone, he had been supported by 200 visitors from his hometown of Hertford in this one. "I won this one for them. They made it seem like a play-off game." He smiled, wiping away the sweat on his brow.

When he beat Milwaukee, 7–2, in his next start, it marked his tenth consecutive complete game. That was on the second Sunday in September. Afterward, when a reporter asked him if he'd be ready to go again two nights later, Hunter looked at him curiously and asked, "Are you kidding?"

The reporter was not, having been briefed by Billy Martin that the manager intended to risk his star's $3,000,000 arm by coming back with him on Sunday with less than his usual three or four days of rest. "We're not out of the race yet," the skipper insisted, his team 11 games back with 13 games remaining.

He didn't mention Cleveland, which was creeping up on the third-place Yankees.

The Cat sat in front of his locker, chewing his Red Man tobacco, spitting it out into a paper cup, and he said, "I can't really tell you why I'm pitching Sunday. You'll have to ask management. But if Billy wants me to, I will. If he wants me to pitch every day, I'll try."

Clearly he did not like it. But he'd do it. He was paid a lot to do what they wanted him to do. So on Sunday he went out and did it. His streak of consecutive complete games was snapped, but he went seven innings, allowed only five hits, didn't walk a man, and the Yankees beat back Cleveland, 6–2, as the Cat's record rose to 22–13.

He might well have made it back to 25 victories again, but the breaks stymied him. He lost in Cleveland, 3–2, then was rained out of a start early in the last week of the season. It rained almost all week in New York, a gloomy ending to a disappointing season.

The skies cleared for the final weekend and on the last Saturday of the season the Yankees swept a double-header to bounce Baltimore out of the running and present the divisional laurels to Boston. Hunter hammered in one of the final nails with a 10-inning 3–2 triumph in one of the games.

This concluded his campaign at 23–14. He had pitched 30 complete games, the most in the majors in 30 years, and 328 innings, leading the big leagues in both categories. He had seven shutouts and a sparking 2.50 earned-run average. Meanwhile, Jim Palmer of Baltimore concluded at

23–11. He had 25 complete games and 310 innings, 10 shut-outs, and a 2.10 ERA.

"He has a lock on the Cy Young Award," said Catfish with a shrug. He was right, too, though perhaps Hunter merited the trophy more.

When the Yankees split a twin bill on the concluding day of the campaign they finished at 83–77, 3½ games ahead of Cleveland, but 7½ games behind Baltimore, and a dozen down to Boston. Where Virdon had compiled a 53–51 mark, Martin managed only a slightly superior 30–26 record.

The 96–65 record with which Boston won the Eastern Division of the American League was not as good as the 98–64 mark with which Oakland won the weak Western Division, but if the A's were good enough to win the divisional laurels without Hunter, they were not good enough to win the postseason play-offs without him, much less the World Series.

Boston swept the A's in three straight to capture the pennant and almost all agreed the series would have been something else had the Catfish been chucking for the Green and Gold, as usual. "With him, we'd have won the opener and kept right on winning. Without him, we didn't expect to win, so we didn't win," one of the A's admitted.

After Boston bowed to Cincinnati in the World Series, another of the A's said, "With Hunter we beat the Reds before and we'd have beaten them again. In the short series, the big pitcher makes the big difference. Charlie lost us our championship when he lost us our big pitcher. A few bucks blew it for us."

Reggie Jackson sighed, held two fingers close together, and said, "We came this close to four straight world championships!"

Finley refused to take the blame for losing. Instead, he pinned it on Dark, who was fired after winning two straight divisional titles, one pennant play-off, and one World Series championship in two seasons, but who'd stood up before a church group and suggested Charlie was going to hell if he did not mend his ways.

As soon as Bill Veeck bought the White Sox and fired

Chuck Tanner, Finley hired him as his latest manager. Tanner still had time left on his Chicago contract, so the hated Sox would have to pay most of his salary, Charlie pointed out proudly. He added that if Tanner couldn't win with the White Sox, he could with the A's . . . with Finley's help.

"It's Hunter's help they need, not Finley's," one of the A's observed. "Dark didn't beat them in 1975. Finley did. Hunter would have won for them, even if he couldn't pull it off for a weaker team."

Hunter may have been the best pitcher in the league. Medich, May, and Dobson were far from it at 14–16, 13–11, and 11–14, respectively, while Lyle was 5–7. Each of the four permitted more than three earned runs per nine innings.

Munson may have been the best catcher in the circuit. He was third in the league with a .318 batting average and fifth with 102 runs batted in. He was the first Yankee to drive home more than 100 runs since Mickey Mantle did it more than 10 years earlier.

Chambliss had personal highs with a .302 batting average and 72 RBI's. Bonds finished fourth in the league with 32 home runs and stole 32 bases, but he hit only .267 and drove in only 78 runs.

No one else contributed consistently. Few played to their potential. Many were far below it.

"The potential of a pennant-winning team is still there," Gabe Paul had decided. "The pitching has to be better. Except for injuries, the attack would have been better. Our balance could be better. We have some weaknesses. We'll have to go into the trade market and try to make some moves. We're not that far from the rest that we can't catch up.

"Last winter's deals should have made the difference, but didn't. Bonds was bothered by a bad leg. I can't complain about Catfish."

Martin said, "Catfish pitched pennant-winning baseball. A few of our players could have played pennant-winning baseball, but didn't. They made a lot of fundamental mistakes. They blew a lot of leads and lost a lot of close games they could have won. The talent is there for this team to win. If we can add to the talent, so much the better. We just have to put it all together."

Which is what baseball men have been saying after bad seasons since baseball began: Wait till next year.

"Next year we may be back in Yankee Stadium," Catfish commented. "That's something to look forward to. For now though, I'm looking forward to the off-season." He was packing up, preparing to pick up his family and head home to Hertford—to his dogs and his hunting and his walks in the woods.

For six months he had lived in the suburbs of the big city. "It wasn't as bad as I thought it might be, but it still isn't the life I like to lead," he observed.

Of course he'd gotten to do television commercials with his dogs and seen his face in advertisements in magazines and newspapers. "It's the place to make money," he conceded. "Making the move here paid off.

"But it was a helluva hectic year. I wouldn't want to go through another year like it. I guess next season will be better. I'm not a novelty anymore. I'll be able to just go out and do my job next season without everyone all over me all the time."

Subsequent developments seemed certain to assure him that.

The impatient Paul plunged into the trade market headfirst over the winter before 1975 even ran out. Instead of hauling in one big Catfish at year's end, he snared a catch of quantity. The Yankee boss dealt Bonds to the Angels in exchange for Mickey Rivers and Ed Figueroa, Dobson to the Indians in exchange for Oscar Gamble, and Medich to the Pirates in exchange for Willie Randolph, Dock Ellis, and Ken Brett.

The Bonds' deal was a shocker. They were still hollering hurrah over him when they suddenly sent him on his way. Considering he played on only one leg, he gave the Yankees super performance in 1975. Clearly, his is a rare talent. But Paul felt he got more than he gave. "Essentially we have swapped power for speed," he said, "and added mound depth."

Rivers at 27 and Randolph at 21 can fly. Rivers led the league with 70 steals in 1975. Gamble can go, too. But the only thing in which he leads the league is hair. Randolph was regarded as potentially a splendid second baseman, but Rivers and Gamble never have been regarded as splendid or enthusiastic outfielders.

Figueroa was regarded as a low-potential pitcher until he won 16 games and allowed an average of less than three earned runs a game for a last-place team in 1975. Ellis and Brett were regarded as high-potential pitchers who did little for a division-leading club at the same time. Ellis, Gamble, and Rivers were regarded as explosive personalities who posed disciplinary problems for the manager.

"Billy can handle players," Paul observed confidently.

"I anticipate no trouble," Martin agreed confidently.

In late December 1975, Martin huddled with Paul to determine if the Yankees were going to enter the bidding for the newest free agents of baseball, Andy Messersmith and Dave McNally. Following the lead of Catfish Hunter, Messersmith and McNally took a different road to the same goal—their freedom—following the 1975 season.

Each played a year beyond his contract, then submitted his request to be declared free of contracts to an arbitration board composed of Marvin Miller, John Gaherin, and Peter Seitz.

Miller, executive director of the Players' Association, voted for the players, as expected. Gaherin, bargaining agent for the owners, voted for the owners, as expected. As in the case of Catfish, the decisive vote was cast for the players by Seitz, a lawyer and professional arbitrator.

Although he had been hired by agreement between the players and owners as an "impartial outsider," Seitz immediately, ludicrously, was dismissed by the owners. An owners' committee announced, "It no longer has confidence in the arbitrator's ability to understand the basic structure of baseball."

Clearly, he had to understand it and interpret it as they did, or they did not want him.

Although he insisted, "I'm no Abe Lincoln freeing the slaves," Seitz's vote struck at the validity of the reserve clause which, with the help of the earlier Congressional ruling, has bound players to any teams which hold their contracts for their complete careers. The owners, of course, promised an extensive court test of the ruling.

Although the owners insisted the game would be ruined if players were free to move from team to team from year to year as their contracts expired, legal experts long have insisted the players were entitled to the same freedoms as other citizens. Presumably, baseball would have to learn to live with it, as other sports are doing these days.

Neither Messersmith nor McNally was a Catfish Hunter, though the talented Messersmith could come close. Neither Messersmith nor McNally could command Catfish's kind of contract. As more players moved into the open market, the bidding was bound to tame down. However, it had become clear that Catfish Hunter had blazed a trail others now would follow. "I didn't want to be a pioneer," he said with a shrug, "just a pitcher."

He would be 30 years of age when the 1976 season started, apparently in his prime and holding his peak. "I'll just try to win 'em all, one at a time, just like always"—he sighed—"if they add up to twenty again, I'll be satisfied.

"If I can help pitch the team to a pennant, I really won't care how many I win," he said.

Was he worth what the others had offered and the Yankees had paid to get him? the Three-Million-Dollar pitcher was asked.

"Since we didn't win the pennant, I guess not," he conceded. "To tell you the truth"—he grinned—"I doubt if any player is worth the sort of money I'm making."

JAMES AUGUSTUS "CATFISH" HUNTER
Born April 8, 1946
Height, 6'0"   Weight, 195 lbs.
Throws and bats right-handed

REGULAR SEASON

SEASON TEAM	G	GS	CG	IP	W	L	SO	BB	ERA
1965 Kansas City	32	20	3	133	8	8	82	46	4.26
1966 Kansas City	30	25	4	177	9	11	109	64	4.02
1967 Kansas City	35	35	13	260	13	17	196	84	2.80
1968 Oakland	36	34	11	234	13	13	172	69	3.35
1969 Oakland	38	35	10	247	12	15	150	85	3.35
1970 Oakland	40	40	9	262	18	14	178	74	3.81
1971 Oakland	37	37	16	274	21	11	181	80	2.96
1972 Oakland	38	37	16	295	21	7	191	70	2.04
1973 Oakland	36	36	11	256	21	5	124	69	3.34
1974 Oakland	41	41	23	318	25	12	143	46	2.49
1975 New York	39	39	30	328	23	14	177	83	2.58

TOTALS (11 yrs.) 402 379 146 2784 184 147 1697 770 —

PLAY-OFFS
1971, 1972, 1973, 1974—seven games, seven starts, two complete games, 51 innings, 3 won, 2 lost, 2.81 ERA.

WORLD SERIES
1972, 1973, 1974—seven games, five starts, two relief, no complete games, 37 innings, 4 won, 0 lost, 2.19 ERA.

NOTES
All games in major leagues (American League).

Led league in victories and earned run average, 1974, and innings pitched and complete games, 1975. Tied for league lead in starts, 1970, and victories, 1975. Second in earned run average, 1975.

Won Cy Young Award as A.L. Pitcher of the Year, 1974. Runner-up for award, 1975.

CODE
G-Games appeared in. GS-Games started. CG-Complete games. IP-Innings pitched. W-Won. L-Lost. SO-Strikeouts. BB-Bases on balls. ERA-Earned run average per nine innings.